CAMPAIGNS
OF
King WILLIAM and Queen ANNE;

From 1689, to 1712.

ALSO,
A New SYSTEM
OF
MILITARY DISCIPLINE,

FOR A
BATTALION of FOOT on ACTION;

With the Most Essential
EXERCISE of the CAVALRY.

Adorn'd with a
MAP of the SEAT of WAR,

AND A
PLAN to the EXERCISE.

By the late *RICHARD KANE*,
GOVERNOR of *Minorca*, and a BRIGADIER-GENERAL.

The Naval & Military Press Ltd

Published by
The Naval & Military Press Ltd
Unit 10 Ridgewood Industrial Park,
Uckfield, East Sussex,
TN22 5QE England
Tel: +44 (0) 1825 749494
Fax: +44 (0) 1825 765701
www.naval-military-press.com

The Naval & Military Press

MILITARY HISTORY AT YOUR FINGERTIPS

... a unique and expanding series of reference works

Working in collaboration with the foremost regiments and institutions, as well as acknowledged experts in their field, N&MP have assembled a formidable array of titles including technologically advanced CD-ROMs and facsimile reprints of impossible-to-find rarities.

In reprinting in facsimile from the original, any imperfections are inevitably reproduced and the quality may fall short of modern type and cartographic standards.

CONTENTS to *Millan*'s SUCCESSION of COLONELS and ESTABLISHMENTS of the NAVY, ARMY and GARRISONS, &c.

Price Thirteen Shillings Bound.

Note. *The Articles mark'd with a* *, *are New to this Edition, and were never printed in any Book before.*

Plate * 1. Generals, Colonels, Lieutenant-Colonels, and Majors, as they rank at this Time in the Army.
*2. Camp Allowance, Rank, Regiments, Field-Officers, and Agents, &c.
Plate 1. to 5. A List of the Horse and Grenadier Guards, Horse-Dragoons, Foot-Guards, Foot and Marines, according to the Rank, or Precedency of each Regiment, with the Colonels to each, from their Rise to this Time —— —— —— *Page* 1 to 20

Plate 6. The same of the Regiments broke in Q. *Anne*'s and K. *George* the Ist's Reigns —— —— —— —— *Page* 21 to 24
Plate 13. An Alphabetical List of all the Colonels (in the said 6 Tables) with Marks to distinguish the Living from the Dead, and Kill'd, with the last, or present Regiment each Colonel had, or have; also the Number of Regiments each had, &c.

ESTABLISHMENT of the NAVY.

Plate 7. and 8. A List of all the Ships in the Royal Navy, with the highest and lowest Number of Men and Guns, Tonnage, Time of Building and Rebuilding, Dimensions in Feet and Inches of each Rate, the Nature of Guns and Shot, Diameter of Bores, * Powder for Proof, Service and Scaling, &c. * Succession of Lord High Admirals, and the Lords Commissioners, from the Year 872 to 1745 —— —— —— —— —— *Page* 25 to 32

Plate 9. * Pay of the Admiralty and Navy Offices. * Ditto in Q. *Elizabeth*'s, K. *James* and King *Charles* the Ist's Times. Pay of the Officers of the Royal Navy. * Pay of the Officers of the Navy and Victualling-Offices, in the Inn and Out-Ports. Officers and Masters at the Royal Academy at *Portsmouth*. 33 to 36

Plate 11. Half Pay of the Officers of the Royal Navy, and the Pensions of their Widows. Distribution of Prizes according to the last Act and Proclamation. * Honours paid to Admiral's Orders for the Marines when on Board, &c. —— *Page* 41 to 44

ESTAB-

ESTABLISHMENT of the ARMY.

Plate 10. Pay and Subsistence, with the Allowance for Recruiting and Cloathing lost by Deserters———*Page* 37. * Pay of the Staff and General Officers, &c. in *Britain, Flanders* and *Ireland*, with all the Deductions from full Pay ——— *Page* 38. * Warrants for Regulating the Army, *viz.* Pay of Dragoons at Winter-Quarters and at Grass. * Pay to, and Deductions from the Foot in Quarters. Prices of all the Commissions in the Army. * Attendance of Foot in Quarters —*Page* 39. * Honours paid to the General Officers, &c. by the Land Forces. * Cloathing the Army, with many other Warrants, all taken from the Originals, with the Dates to each that the King signed them. *Page* 40

Plate 11. Half Pay of the Officers and Pensions of the Widows of the Army. * General Estimate of the *British, Hanoverian, Hessian* and *Irish* Forces, at Home and Abroad, with their Numbers and Pay —*Page* 41. * Succession of the Captains to the Band of Gentlemen Pensioners, with their various Pay and Numbers, from their Rise to this Time. * The same of the Yeomen of the Guards.— *Page* 42. Fees from all the Officers in the Army at their taking their Commissions, to the Secretaries of State, War and Commissaries Office. * Last Order for Cloathing the Army ——*Page* 43. * Muster of the Houshold in Bands of Horse before *Edward* VI. * Marine Orders. * Honours to Field-Marshals. A Table to compute Salaries, from one eighth of a Penny, to 2000*l.* from one Day to 365 Days. ——*Page* 44

Plate 12. *British* Garrisons *Irish* and *Plantation* Garrisons — Names of Governors, and Lieutenant Governors, &c. — *Page* 45, 6, 7 — *Page* 48

To which is added,

Plate 14. A List of the * *Hanoverian* and * *French* Armies, as they stand in Rank; their Antiquity, Number of Squadrons or Battalions, and Pay; with that of the *Hessians* and *Danes, viz.* of General and other Officers and private Men, *per* Day, in *English* Money.

Plate 15. Garrisons and Towns of War, &c. in 1538.

N. B. This Edition is as Compleat as I can possibly make it; and with Sheets that come to 2*s.* 6*d.* every Year, it may be good forever.

Sold by the said J. MILLAN, Bookseller, opposite the *Admiralty-Office, Whitehall.*

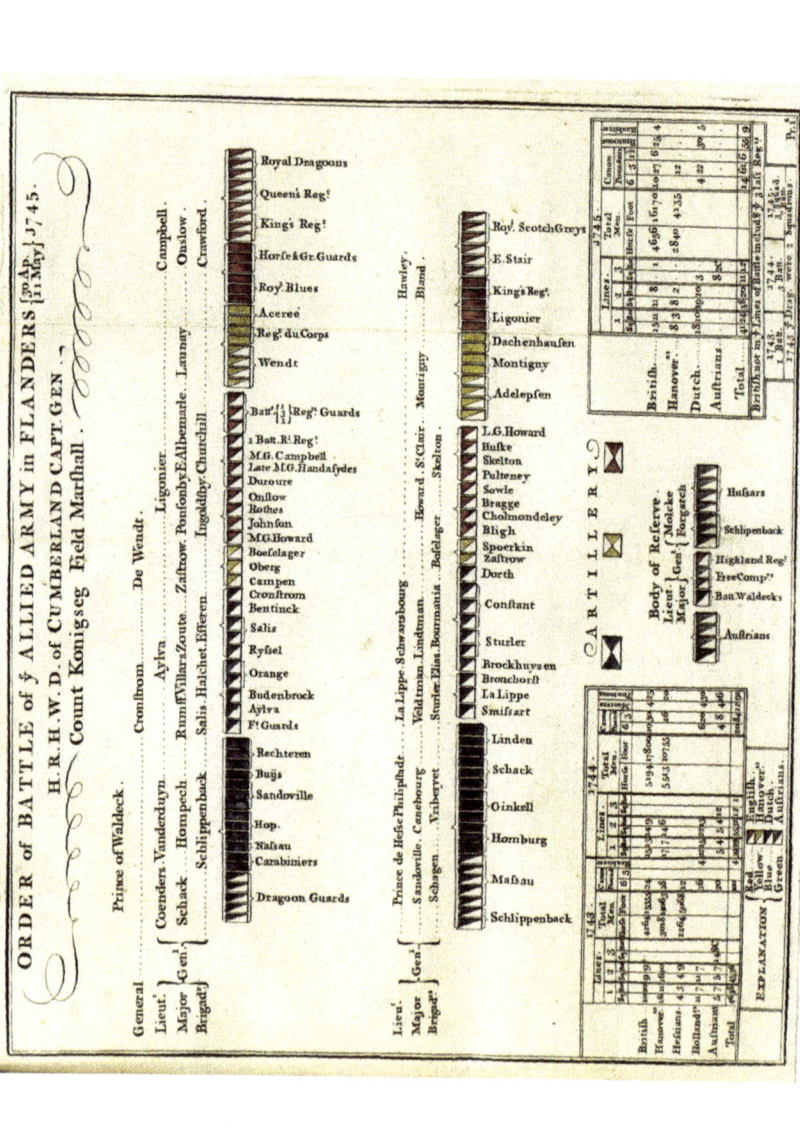

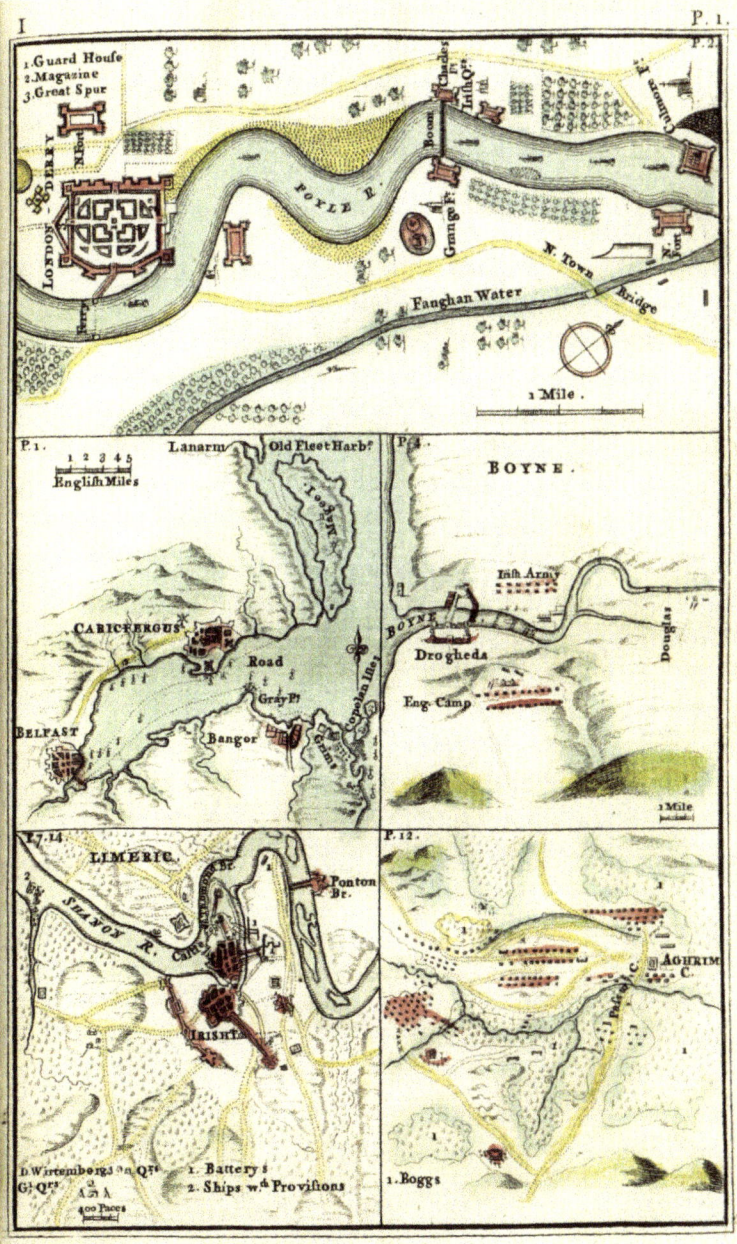

NAMUR as TAKEN 20 Ast 1695.

1 English Mile

a Ld Cuts	Assault at } Breach of y^e	f Terra Nova Cohorn	p. Brussells }	y Lower Town
b Riveriss			q. Iron } Gate	z Retrenchm^t } Attack'd 8 J^y
c La Caves			r. St Nicholas }	& Stone Line } in ye Siege
d Swerins	Assault } at ye Cassottes &c	k Castle	s. Lines of Com^{un}.	1 Stone Line
e Eng. } Aproaches		l City	t	2 Terra Nova
f Dutch } for Trenches		m Cassot } Fort	u. } Lodge- } ments } made	
g		n Cohorn }	v.	
h Batteries		o Demi Bastion	w. }	
i Bridge of Com^{un}.			x. }	

Castle wth Cohorn in y^e Siege
by y^e Eng. & Dutch 17 J^y
on y^e Demi Bast^n 23 J^y
w^n we took y^e Stone Line after y^e Assault 20 Ast

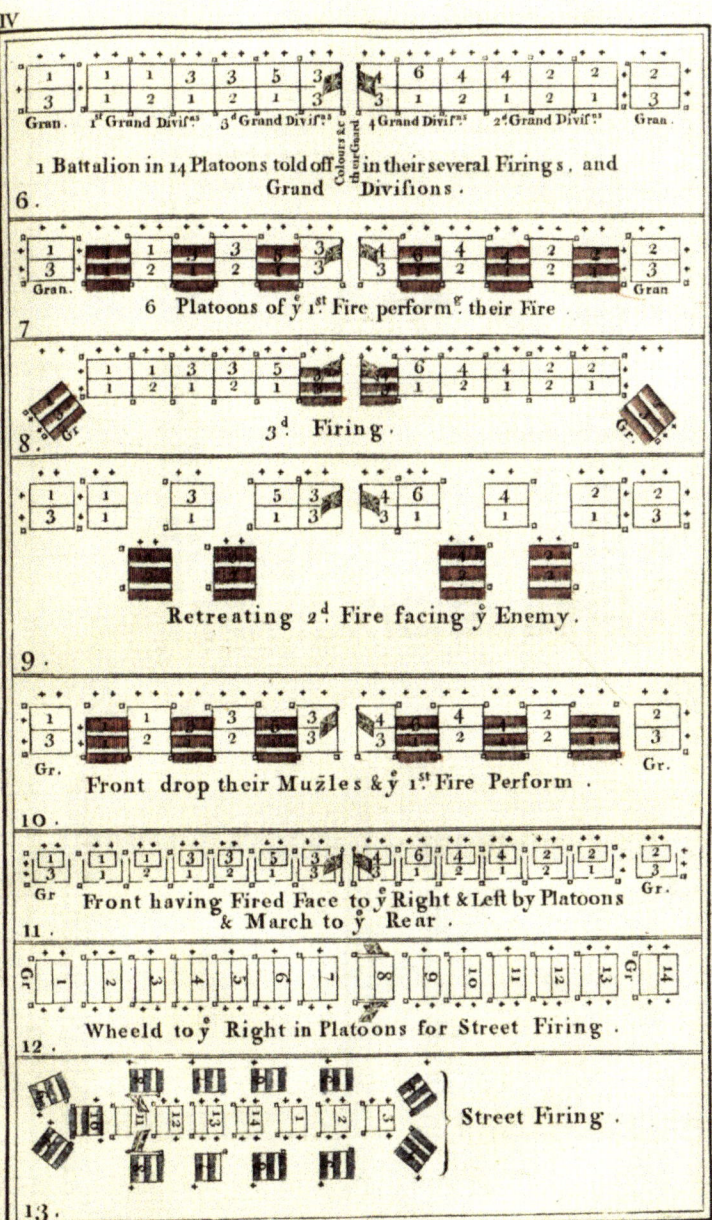

IV

6. 1 Battalion in 14 Platoons told off in their several Firings, and Grand Colours &c the Grand Divisions.

7. 6 Platoons of y̆ 1ˢᵗ Fire perform.ᵍ their Fire.

8. 3ᵈ Firing.

9. Retreating 2ᵈ Fire facing y̆ Enemy.

10. Front drop their Muzles & y̆ 1ˢᵗ Fire Perform.

11. Front having Fired Face to y̆ Right & Left by Platoons & March to y̆ Rear.

12. Wheeld to y̆ Right in Platoons for Street Firing.

13. Street Firing.

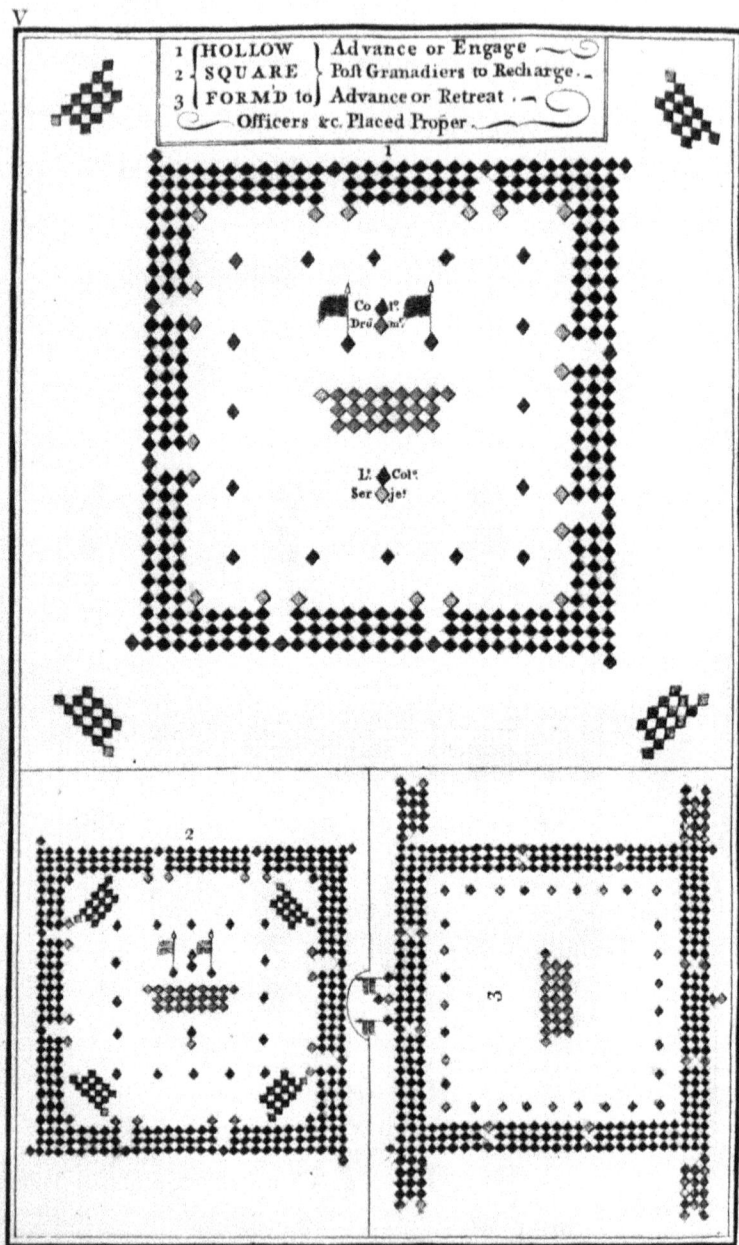

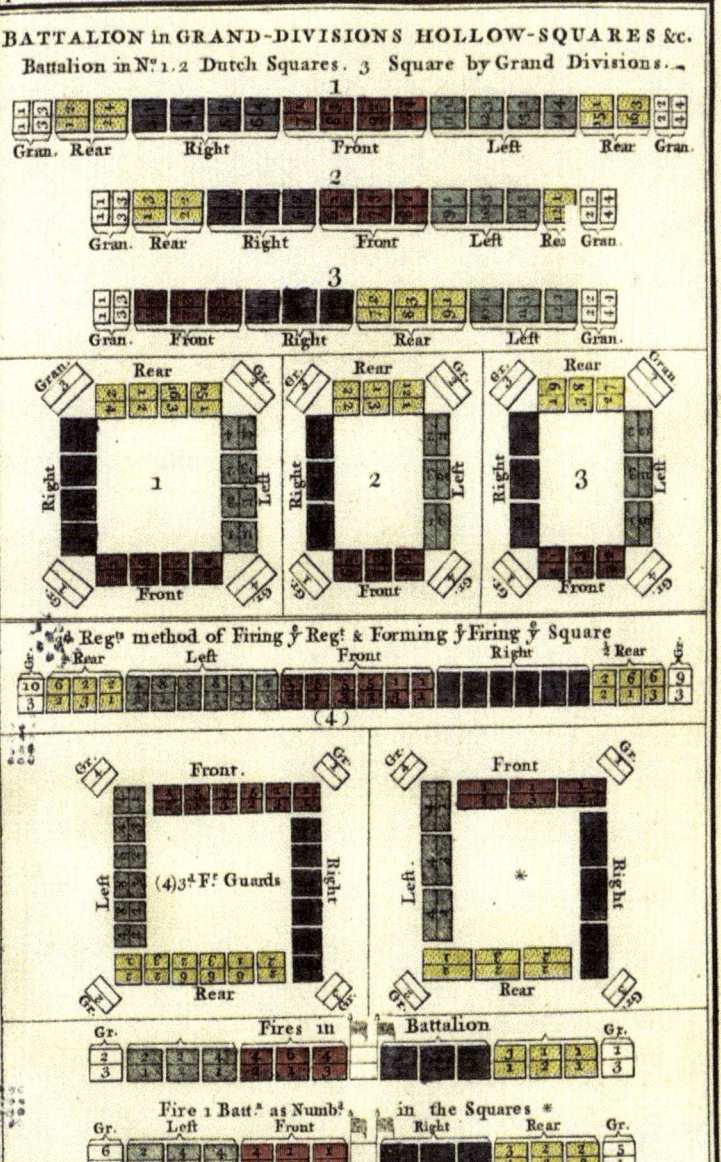

HOLLOW-SQUARE ATTACK'D
By HORSE on all Sides.

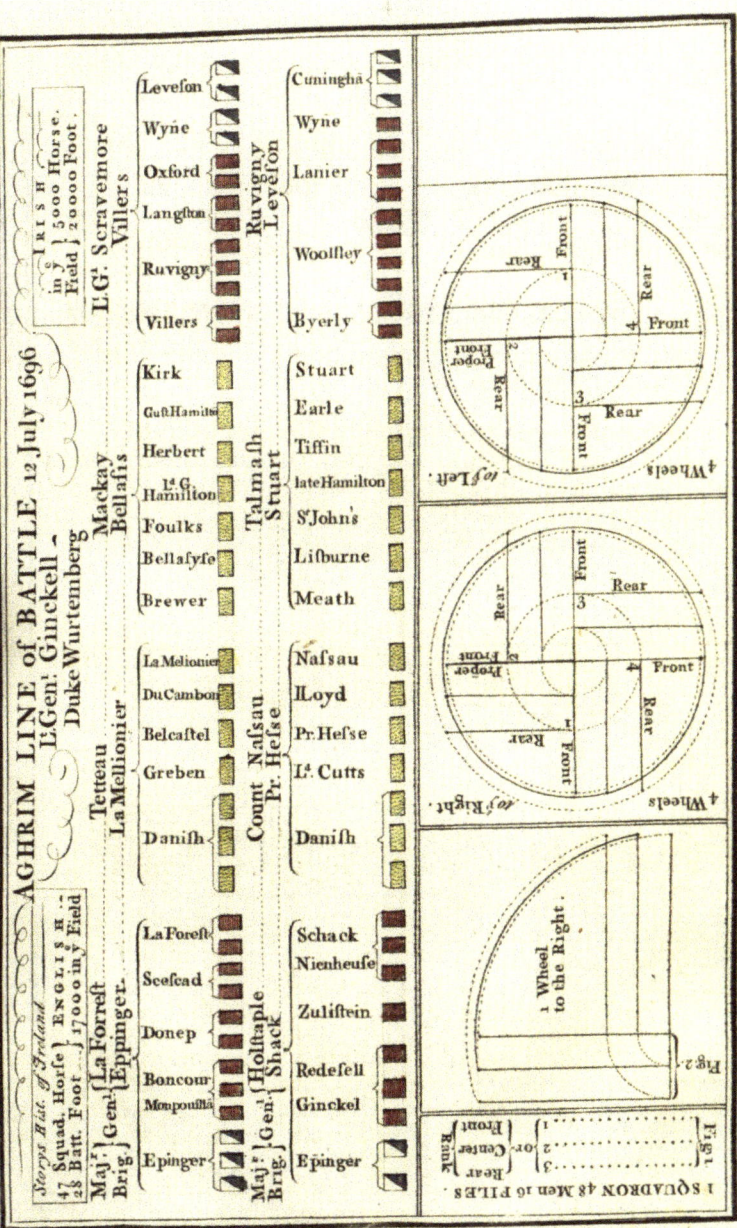

XI.

BATTALION making its 3 FIRINGS

A																	
B																	
C																	
D																	

1, 2 & 3 Firings Answer thus: 15, 1, 9, 3, 11, 5, 13, 7, 17, 18, 8, 14, 6, 12, 4, 10, 2, 16

Return of ẏ Regt. of Foot Comanded by

Officers						Staff Officers					Serjts Drum		Rank & File							Since last Return			
Colonel	Lt. Col.	Major	Capts.	Lieuts.	Ensigns	Chaplain	Adjut.	Q.Mr.	Surgeon	Surg.Mate	Serjeants	Drumers	Corporals	Centinels	Furlo	Party	Recruits	Sick	Effective	Defective	Entertain'd	Dismiss'd	Deserted	Dead

Strength of his Majesty's 1. Regimt. of Foot Guards

Officers &c. Present							Rank & File		Officers Absent					
Field Officers	Captains	Lieuts.	Ensigns	Serjeants	Corporals	Drumers	Centinels	Wanting to Comp.	Colonel	Lt.Col.	Major	Captains	Lieuts.	Ensigns
4	24	32	24	84	84	55	1979	9						

Return of Lt.Co. — Troop of ẏ Honbl.Co. — Regt. of Horse

					Born		Listed			Furlo or Recruit			Bought				
Name	Age	Size	Complex	County	Town	by	when	Trade			Age	Size	by	when	Mark	No.	Ailment

MEN   **HORSES**

REGIMT. DRAGOONS REVIEW'D 26 Agst. 1745 by Genl.

Field Officers & Captains	Absent	Serv'd Years	Lieuts.	Absent	Serv'd	Cornets	Absent	Serv'd	Q.Mrs.	Absent	Serv'd Years	Serjeants	Corporals	Drums	Hautbois	P. Men	Sick		on Furlo	Total		Want to Comp		
																	Men	Horses		Men	Horses	Men	Horses	Reason
Col:J.		9	Cap.Lt.C		6	R.			J.		1													
Lt.Co.C.		3	L.		7	Y.			T.		7													
Majr. H.		8	A.		5	C.			Y.		2													
Captain N.		5	N.		8	H.			M.		6	12	2	2	1	57				65	65			
Captain M.		7	M.		3	A.			J.		3													
Captain J.		6	A.		9	R.			L.		5													
Total 6			6			6			6			12	12	12										

Chaplain Adjutt. Surgeon & Mates Reckond.   Arms &c. their Condition
Officers or Men if Absent, ẏ Reason why.   Bad Horses to be Exchang'd or Sold
Qr. Clear'd every Month. Complaints   Dragoons Exercis'd as Horse or Foot
redress'd at all times.   Reported to ẏ Commissary Gl. &c.

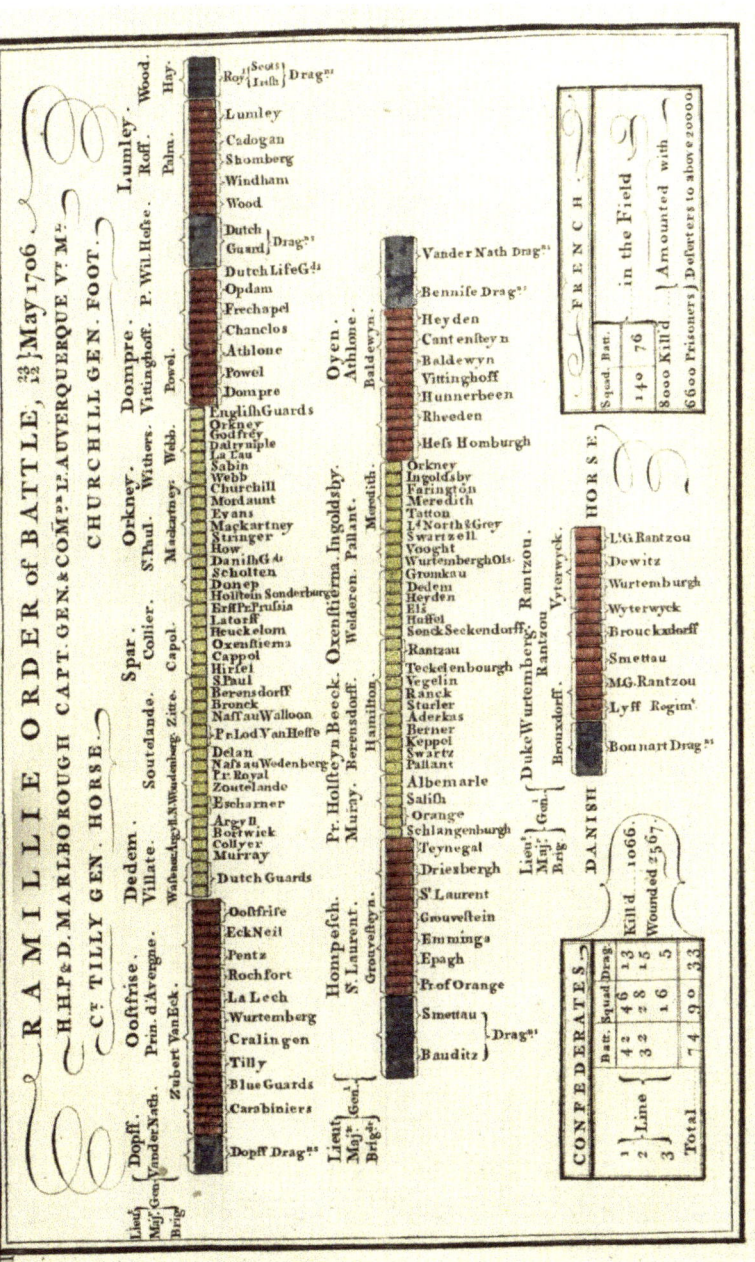

ENCAMPMENTS, WINTER QUARTERS, MARCHES, STRENGTH &c. from 1701 to 1713 of the ALLIES / FRENCH

		In y^e Field				In Garrison				Time Marchd			Battles Sieges & Camps	Generals & Comand	Forces		Ordnance			Generals & Comand	Forces		Ordnance		
	Country	Weeks	Days	Begun Ended		Weeks	Days	Begun	Ended	Years	Weeks	Days	Days	Leagues	Miles			Bataillon	Squad^ds	Canon	Mortars	Pontoons		Bataillon	Squad^ds	Canon	Mortars	Pontoons
1701	Brabant	6	1	7 June 22	18 23											ber K.W. Breda 21	K. for our Camp	12	290	20	—	—	Bois le D.	80	150	92	21	32
1702	D^s & Quart	33	5	9 Mar. 31	24	2	27 8b^r	9 Mar.				29	3	24	216	648	Breda 21 ber K.W. Kayserwort Camp							D.Burgundy & M.Mar.Pusee	76	120	62	8	24
																Duckenberg 26 June	Hindlow	84	150	92	21	40	D^c.&M.Vilr.	94	92	88	16	24
1703	in Breda	27	4	19	27	25	5	27	24 Apr			1		6	43	140 420	Pier Canonad 8 Ag^t												
																Maestricht 6 May	M. Overkerque	70	140	80	20	32	Mar^l Villars						
1704	Germ & z D	30	24	20.9b 20		4				1		4	94	144	432	Valnotrel. S. Ag^t 4 offin. Gingen 16 June &c Hochstet B. 2 Ag.	Marlb & Pr.Eug.	74	140	90	—	—	Man^s Villars					
																	Marlb & Baden	96	202	44	—	24	D^c Bavaria	88	160	90	40	30
1705	[on ye Brmb Breda]	27	5	20 9b 31		25	3	31	27	1			66	147	26	Elist 24 May Ft. Lines forc'd 7 July	Marlbro	84	26	52	8	24	D^c C Tal^d	87	160	90	40	30
																							Marq Villars	106	160	80	60	24	36
1706		26	2	27	28 8b 27	28	5 May 11 May			1	1		39	132	396	Ramelies B. 12 May	Marlbro	108	166	60	24	36						
1707		24	5	5 Apr	29	1	09	11 May		1			25	90	270	Helsheim & 4 July &c	Overqueen	98	156	—	20	—	Villeroy	76	132	66	12	36
1708	Flanders	32	5	11	26 De 25			6 Jun.		1	1	5	41	129	387	Meldart 21 May Oudenard B. 30 June S. Lisle 31 Ag.	Marlbro	102	210	108	24	44	D^c Bavaria	90	150	80	16	—
1709		19	3	6 Jun	20 8b 23			8b	3	1			28	82	246	Tournay S. 6 June Malplaquet B. 31 Ag.	Marlb & Eugen	131	241	104	44	42	Vendom & Bavaria	112	180	108	12	36
1710	& Ghent	31	6	3	29 E. 21	4	29	9b	12 Ap	1	1	2	32	85	255	Douay S. 7 July Lewarl S. 12 May	Marlb & Eugen	155	262	204	30	48	Marq. Villars	104	200	96	16	36
1711		27	6	24	24	23	1	24	5	1			34	94	282	Lantz 3 June	Marlbro	119	226	134	41	11	Marq. Villars	193	248	90	12	32
1712		25	6	Apr 3	8b 35			8b	3	3			19	60	180	Sollem 16 May Landrefie S. 10 July	D^c Ormond	132	204	—	12	—	Vendom	148	292	100	16	36
	Some Esq in Ghent to 1716.									4	3	8	12	12	36	6 July Allies left by		24	25	66	10	18		150	300	—	—	—
12 Campaigns 312 6 or 6 Years Camp 302 6 or 6 Years in Garrs 12 1												500	1832	5596														

A Bataillon in 18 Platoons, told off in 3 Firings, 4 Men Deep, 2 Kneel, 2 Stand

A Bataillon making its several Firings.

First Fire | 5 Set | Fire 6 |
Third | 6 Fire | 4 |
Reserve or Fourth Fire.

Platoons } Right By either Motion a Reg^ts gains or
File to ye Left lest w^y ground of 1 Platoon.

XV

INCAMPMENT for a BATTALION of 10 or 13 Companies

Quart⸱Guard

Parade Line

Line for 10 Companies

Colours · · · & Drums
Bells for   Arms

6   Dou — ble   Str — eets   for
Ser — je — ants — &Pri — vate — Men   Granadiers

Subalterns

Captains

Major   Lt. Col.

Colonel

Staff   Officers

Grooms & Horses

Grand   Sutlers

Paces
10 20 30 40 50 60 70 80 90 100

CAPT.s of y.e RIGHT WING 1709 — COLONELS, Lt. COLs. MAJORS, and

N.o	1	2	3	4	5	6	7	8	9	10	11	12	13	14	15	16	17	18	19	20	21	22	23	24	25
British 44																									
Prussians 18																		17							
Hanover 14										10															
									9																

SUBALTERNS at TOURNAY 1709 — CAPTAINS and

N.o	1	2	3	4	5	6	7	8	9	10	11	12	13	14	15	16	17	18	19	20	21	22	23	24	25
British 44																									
Prussians 9								9																	
Hanover 20												4													
Dutch 30													2												

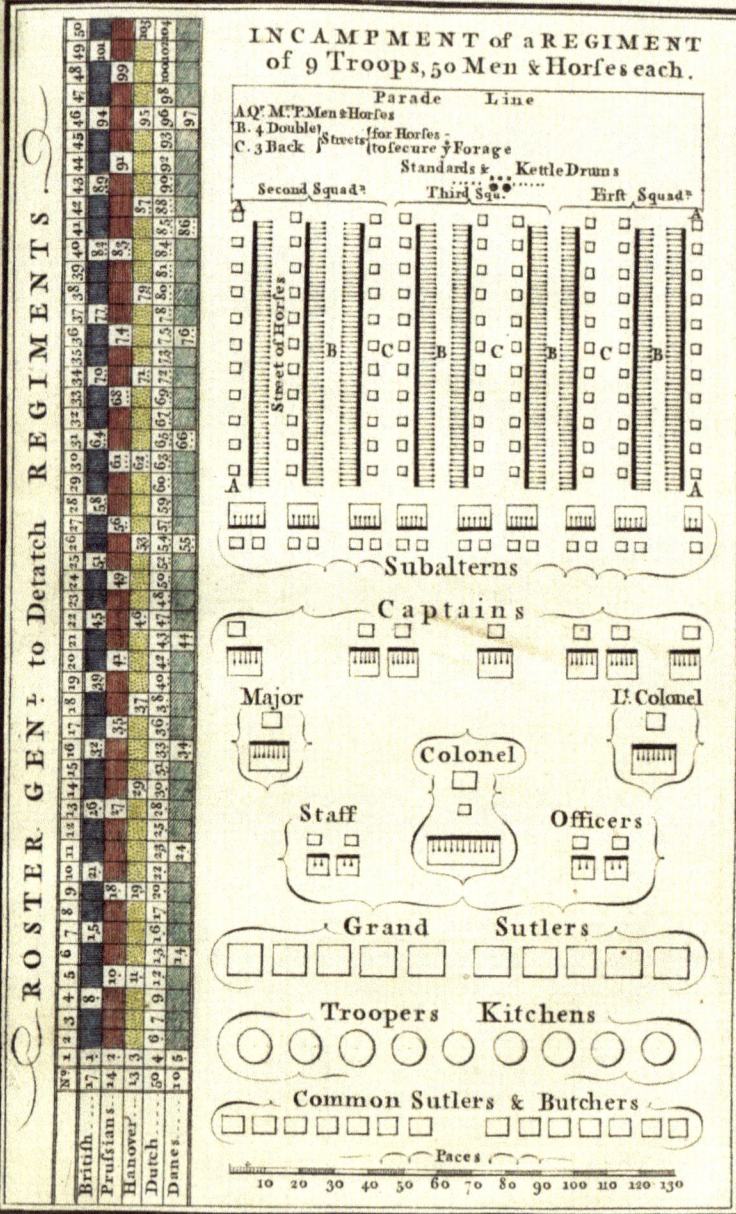

MEMOIRS

OF ALL THE

CAMPAIGNS of King *William*

IN

Ireland and in *Flanders*, &c.

HE Regiment of Foot that I serv'd in, is well known by the Title of the *Royal Regiment* of *Ireland*, from which Regiment I may without Vanity say, our *British* Infantry had the Ground-work of their present Discipline.

IN *August*, 1689, the above Regiment sail'd from *High-Lake* in *Cheshire*, under the Command of Duke *Schomberg*, landed near *Belfast* in *Ireland*, and march'd from thence to *Carrick-Fergus*, to which Place we laid Siege, the Duke having between 12 or 14,000 Men in his Army. *Carrick-Fergus* surrender'd in a few Days after we came before it, with little Loss on either Side.

1689.

A   King

1689. King *James*, at this Time, was in Possession of the whole Kingdom, except *Londonderry* and *Enniskilling*, whither the Protestants fled, and defended those Places to a Miracle. Upon the Duke's landing, he was drawing the *Irish* Army together, about *Dundalk*, but upon our advancing thither, he retir'd to *Ardee*. It was the 9th of *September* when we came to *Dundalk*, which the Duke finding to be a strong Pass, with a pretty good Haven for small Ships to bring him Necessaries from *England*, and the *Newry-Mountains* just in his Rear, which secur'd him behind, and kept open a Communication with the North, where he propos'd to take up his Winter-Quarters, and be supplied from thence with fresh Provisions; whereupon he resolv'd to advance no farther, but fix here for the remaining Part of the Campaign. He therefore incamp'd on the North Side of the River and Town; he immediately caused that Part of the Town which lay towards the Enemy, to be well fortify'd, and also threw up a strong Intrenchment from the River to the Mountain, which secur'd the Right Flank of our Camp, and from all Attempts of the Enemy: Having thus secur'd himself on all Sides, he gave Orders for the Army to halt. Our *Dutch* and *French* Regiments soon built themselves good warm Barracks, but our *English* Regiments being all raw Soldiers, and not knowing the Consequence of not Hutting, neglected till there was neither Timber nor Straw to be had, so that when the rainy Weather came on, our Men died like rotten Sheep. About a Week after our coming thither, Major-General *Kirk* joined us with two Regiments of Foot, which he had brought from *England* for the Relief of *Londonderry*, and also by 1500 Men from *Iniskilling*, which made our Army about 16,000.

King

King William, *in* Ireland *and in* Flanders.

King *James* headed the *Irish* Army at *Ardee*, 1689-90 which was more than double our Number, among whom were 7000 *French*, from whom there came over to us several Deserters, who took Service in our *French* Regiments, as *Hugonets*, but were in Reality *Papists*, sent to inveigle our *French*; among whom were many *Papists*. The Manner of our mounting the Intrenchment that extended from the River to the Mountain, was, every Evening by Brigades, and drew off in the Morning, and there being three *French* Regiments of Foot, they made up one Brigade. Now these Deserters in a little Time had brought over a considerable Number to join in betraying the Camp to the Enemy, when it should come to the Turn of their Brigade to mount the Intrenchment; at which Time they would find Means by changing and chopping with others, (which is a Thing too common among the Soldiers, and ought not to be suffered,) that most of those Confederates were to be on this Command, and then they were to give Notice to the Enemy, who were to be in Readiness to march and fall upon us by Break of Day, which they might easily have done, being but at eight Miles Distance; but this Affair was happily discovered, and by some of the *Protestants* that had been let into the Secret, on which five of the Ringleaders were hang'd, (one of them was actually a Captain in the *French* with King *James*) and between 2 and 300 sent Prisoners to *England*. Thus was this small Army providentially preserv'd, not above two Days before the Thing was to be put in Execution. About the latter End of *September* King *James*, at the Head of his Army, march'd from *Ardee*, and drew up on a Rising Ground about a Mile from us, expecting the Duke would draw out, and give him Battle; but when he found we kept within our Works,

Works, after about an Hour's Halt, he march'd back to his Camp, where he continued till the Beginning of *November*, at which Time he broke up, and went into Winter-Quarters. While we lay at *Dundalk*, the Weather proving very Rainy, and our Men being ill Hutted, the Country Distemper got among them to that Degree, that more than two Thirds of our *English* were carried off by it. 1690. In the Beginning of *June* King *William* landed near *Belfast*, and gave Orders for assembling the Army at *Dundalk*, which was computed to be something more than 30,000. King *James* at this Time was drawing his Army together, along the Banks of the *Boyne* near to *Drogheda*, who were much about our Number. On the last Day of *June*, our King advanc'd with his Army up to the Enemy, and encamp'd within Cannon Shot of them.

As the King was this Evening taking a View of the Enemy, having stopt too long in a Place, a Cannon-Ball graz'd on his Shoulder, which rais'd a small Contusion, however did not hinder him from acting the next Day, being the First of *July*, when he drew up the Army in Order of Battle; but observing the Enemy drawn up in great Order along the River, he saw it would be a difficult Task to pass it, unless he could oblige them to break the Disposition they had made; wherefore he ordered Lieutenant-General *Douglas*, with about 8000 Men to march about two Miles up the River, and there to pass in order to fall upon their Left Flank. This answer'd the King's Expectation; for when they saw *Douglass* marching that Way, they immediately sent off a great Part of their Left Wing to oppose him. By which their Order of Battle was broke, and their whole Army put into Motion to make good the Ground of their Left Wing; which the King observing, march'd down

down immediately, and entered the River while they were in this Motion; so that before they form'd, he got over his Front Line and engag'd them, and the second being close at the Heels of them, got soon over to the Assistance of the first; and in a short Time after the Enemy was put to Flight, before *Douglas* could come to engage their Left.

King *James* had posted himself on a rising Ground in the Rear of his Army, who, as soon as he saw our Troops pass the River, was the first that fled, and never look'd behind him till he got to *Duncanon* Fort, from whence he sailed to *France*. The Loss of the Enemy did not amount to more than 1000 kill'd, and about as many taken. The greatest Loss on our Side, was, the brave Duke *Schomberg*, who was kill'd (as it was said, by a *French* Trooper that had serv'd in his own Regiment, and deserted while we lay at *Dundalk* the preceding Year) in the 84th Year of his Age. The *Irish*, in a dispersed Manner, made the best of their Way to the *Shannon*.

The *French* Troops, with some of the Horse kept together till they pass'd the *Shannon* at *Athlone*, from whence they march'd to *Galloway*, where they waited till Shipping came and carried them to *France*. However, the *Irish* resolved to defend the *Shannon*, and stand out till they could hear from their King; they therefore drew all their shatter'd Troops to *Limerick* and *Athlone*. The next Day after the Battle the King marched the Army towards *Dublin*, where we halted a few Days, until he had settled the Government; after which he sent Lieutenant-General *Douglass* with Part of the Army towards *Athlone*, to try if he could secure that Post, whilst the King himself march'd with the rest of the Army towards *Limerick*, and was join'd by *Douglass* the Day before he arriv'd;

having been prevented by Lieutenant-General *Sarsfield*, who had rallied Part of the Enemy at *Athlone*.

On the First of *August*, the King sate down before *Limerick*, which the River *Shannon* divides into two Parts: The Enemy had secur'd themselves on *Thumond* Side the Water, which prevented the King from investing the Town round, and was oblig'd to carry on the Siege against that Part of it that lay on our Side the River; we soon open'd our Trenches, took an advanced Work, and were raising Batteries against the Arrival of our Battering-Train, which was on the Road from *Dublin*; of which the Enemy having an Account, and of the slender Guard that was with it, they sent *Sarsfield* with a strong Body of Horse, who passing the *Shannon* at *Killalo*, fell on the Train the 11th of *August* about Midnight, as they lay at *Cullen*, within eleven Miles of our Camp, where they burnt and destroy'd every Thing that could be useful to us. This was a well-manag'd Affair of *Sarsfield*'s, and would have redounded much to his Honour, had he not sullied it with so much Cruelty; for tho' there was not the least Opposition, yet he put Man, Woman, and Child to the Sword. The King had some Account of *Sarsfield*'s Motion, and sent Sir *John Lanier* to march with a good Body of Horse to join the Train at *Cullen*; but Sir *John* delay'd the Time, and did not march till several Hours after his Orders, and loiter'd even on his March, by making unnecessary Halts; which gave *Sarsfield* Time to do his Business, and return without the Loss of a Man. Sir *John*, who had once been a great Favourite of King *James*'s, was shrewdly suspected of Treachery: The King only cashier'd him, whereas he ought to have been hang'd.

Notwithstanding the Loss of the Train, the King push'd on the Siege with the Train he had, with
which

King William, *in* Ireland *and in* Flanders.

which a confiderable Breach was made in the Wall, 1690. and one of the Towers batter'd down; whereupon he order'd an Affault to be made by moſt of the Grenadiers in his Army, and to be fuſtain'd by 17 Plattoons, of whom our Regiment was one. The Lord *Cutts* led on the Grenadiers, who inſtead of mounting the Breach, follow'd the Enemy that fled along the Covert-way, which drew the Battalions after him, ſo that the Breach was neglected, by which the Affair miſcarried. Our Regiment upon this Occaſion had one Lieutenant-Colonel, one Captain, and five Subalterns kill'd, beſides one wounded. The King meeting with theſe Diſappointments before *Limerick*, drew off (the 30th of *Auguſt*) and leaving the Army under the Command of Lieutenant-General *Gingkill*, he went to *Waterford*, from whence he ſail'd to *England*.

Upon our marching off from *Limerick*, Part of the Army were ſent under the Command of the Duke of *Wirtemberg*, to aſſiſt the Lord *Churchill* in the taking *Cork* and *Kinſale*, the reſt of the Army were diſpers'd into Quarters, ſo as to form a Frontier againſt the *Shannon*.

In *May*, General *Gingkill* drew the Army toge- 1691. ther near *Mullingar*, which was computed to be near 24,000. The firſt Place we march'd againſt was *Ballimore*, a Frontier the Enemy had, half-way between *Mullingar* and *Athlone*: this Place being ſituated in an Iſland, in a Lough, held out eight Days. From whence we march'd to *Athlone*, which is divided by the *Shannon*, as that of *Limerick*; that Part of the Town which lay on our Side of the River we took the third Day we came before it; but the other Part was ſtrongly fortify'd with a large ſtrong Tower in the Middle of it, that overlook'd our Part of the Town; and along this deep and rapid River they had thrown up a double Intrenchment, and with all their Army, confisting of 27,000, lay incamp'd within half a Mile on the Back of the Town, commanded by *St. Ruth*, a *French* General of great Experience. Notwithstanding these Difficulties, our General feem'd resolv'd to push at this Place, tho' the Generality of the Army thought it a very hazardous Undertaking.

We first threw up a very large strong Intrenchment close to the River below the Bridge, on which Batteries were rais'd for 50 Pieces of Cannon, besides Mortars, with which we foon batter'd down the Face of the Tower that lay next us, and in a manner levell'd the outward Trench along the River; but this avail'd little, unlefs the River was fordable, which never happens but in a dry Seafon, and this proving fo, our General wanted to know the Depth of the Water: three *Danish* Soldiers, who for fome Crime lay under Sentence of Death, to whom the General offer'd Pardon, and a Gratuity, if they would ford the River; which they readily accepted, and putting on Armour, they enter'd the River at Noon-Day, keeping at fome Diftance from each other: fome of our Men in the Trenches were order'd to fire as it were at them, but over their Heads, which made the Enemy believe they were Deferters, fo did not fire a Shot at them till they had pafs'd the Depth of the River, and faw them returning, at which Time they began to fire at them; but our great and fmall Shot being prepared for that Purpofe, fired with fuch Fury upon them, that they were not able to hold up their Heads: fo the Men return'd with only two of 'em flightly wounded. When the General found the River paffable, he refolv'd on making a general Affault, for which he gave Orders, that 40 Grenadiers out of each Company, and 80 choice Men out of each

each Regiment, should be ready to march down the next Morning, in order to make the Attack.

1691.

This Detachment march'd openly about Ten in the Morning into our Works, at which time all the Hills on our Side were cover'd with Spectators to behold this Action: this brought *St. Ruth* with his whole Army down to the Back of the Town, and crowded it with as many Men as it could well hold.

This put the General off making the Assault; so towards Evening he order'd the Detachments to march back to Camp, but at the same time gave strict Orders, that neither Officers nor Soldiers should be put upon any other Duty, or stir from their Regiments, but be ready to turn out at a Minute's Warning. *St. Ruth* seeing our Detachment drawing off, return'd with his Army to Camp, satisfy'd, that our General would lay aside all Thoughts of passing the *Shannon* at this Place.

That Night and the next Day we did not fire a Shot, nor make Show of any Design of a Siege; so that a Rumour was spread thro' both Camps, that our General finding it not possible to pass the *Shannon* here, was for marching to *Banahar*, to try what he could do there. This confirm'd *St. Ruth* in the Notion he had conceiv'd; whereupon he invited all the Ladies, and Generals of his Camp, to an Entertainmentt on the 22d, the Day our General design'd to make his real Attack, the other being only a Feint.

Our General early this Morning plac'd Centinels on all the Hills, to prevent People appearing on them; and about Ten o'Clock there came Orders along the Line for the Detachment to draw out, and march into our Works with all the Privacy imaginable; which we perform'd with that Exactness, that the Enemy did not suspect what we were about, but

rather

1691. rather thought we were drawing off our Cannon, till about Two o'Clock, we on a sudden bounc'd over our Works, and were got a good Way into the River before they perceiv'd us; who being, as it were, rous'd out of Sleep in the greatest Consternation, and the Cannon and small Shot from our Trenches firing with great Fury over our Heads, struck them with such a Pannick, that they made little or no Resistance; and before *St. Ruth* had any Account of the Attack, we were Masters of the Town, but not the Castle. This, one may believe, spoil'd the Entertainment. *St. Ruth* got his Army under Arms, and march'd down with all the Expedition he could, in order to drive us back; but he discover'd a grand Mistake which he had committed, too late to be remedied; for, having left the Works of the Back-Part of the Town standing, they now became a Bulwark against himself, nor could he pretend to force us thence but by carrying on a formal Siege: so that he was obliged to march back with his Army, and leave us in Possession of the Town; and early next Morning he decamp'd, and march'd off in some Disorder; at which time those in the Castle surrendred at Discretion, wherein were a Major-General, a Brigadier, and near 1000 Men, besides 1000 kill'd: We had but 29 Men kill'd, and as many wounded; not an Officer of Note hurt.

Here the old Proverb was verify'd, that *Security dwells next Door to Ruin*. *St. Ruth* thought it impossible for us to pass the River before he could be down with the Army; and it is most certain nothing but Neglect of their Duty was the Occasion of it: which may serve as a very good Lesson for Officers in general never to think themselves secure on any Post or Guard, if the Commanding Officer neglects his Post, (as it was here) all under him will do the same;

King William, *in* Ireland *and in* Flanders. 11

same; for they seeing their General secure in himself, thought all was safe, which made them neglect keeping their Men strictly on their Duty, and having a vigilant Eye on us. Had they done thus, it would have been impossible for us to march but they might easily see us from the Castle, and give timely Notice to their General, which would have prevented what follow'd: But all being thus lull'd in Security when we made this unexpected Attack, it was such a Surprize on them, that they rather threw down their Arms, and ran for it, than made any thing of a gallant Resistance, which appears by the Kill'd on both Sides. The great Oversight *St. Ruth* committed, in leaving the Works on the Back-Part of the Town standing, was the only Motive that induced our General to pass the *Shannon* at this Place.

1691.

Two Days after this Action our Army passed the River, and encamp'd near the Ground where the Enemy had lain; and when we had clean'd the Town, and repair'd the Works, we march'd after the Enemy. Our first Day's March was to *Ballynasloe*, where the General had an Account, that the Enemy was strongly encamp'd at *Aughrim* within three Miles of us, and waited for our coming.

Next Morning being *July* 12, our General sent all our Tents and Baggage back to *Athlone*, and march'd in four Columns up to them, where we found them in Order of Battle, with their whole Camp standing at a small Distance in their Rear; which look'd as if they were resolv'd to win the Day, or lose all. Their Right was cover'd with a Bogg, which extended along their Front, till it passed their Centre; from whence were a Parcel of old Garden-Ditches, which extended to the Castle of *Aughrim*, and cover'd their Left Flank,

Here

1691. Here *St. Ruth* seem'd resolv'd to die, or recover the Honour he had lost at *Athlone*; and indeed he made an excellent Disposition of his Army, and was very active in giving his Orders, and seeing his Troops do their Duty in all Parts.

Our General began the Battle about Four in the Afternoon, by attacking them on the Right, and so gradually on, till our Right (where was our Regiment) engaged those on their Left, that lined the Garden-Ditches. Our Troops, that engaged their Right and Centre, were hard put to it for a considerable Time; and were several times repuls'd, the Enemy having maintain'd their Ground in those Parts with great Resolution: But those posted in the Ditches did not behave so well; when we on the Right attack'd, they gave us their Fire, and ran to the next Ditches, and we scrambling over the first Ditch, made after them to the second; from whence they gave us another scattering Fire, and ran to other Ditches behind them, we still pursuing from one Ditch to another, until we had drove them out of four or five Rows of those Ditches into an open Plain, where was some of their Horse drawn. In climbing those Ditches, and still following them from one to another, no one can imagine we could keep our Order: In this Hurry there were Battalions so intermingled together, that we were at a Loss what to do; and certainly their Horse would have made fine Work with us, if our Horse had not found Means to get round into the Plain, and engage those of the Enemy: and here we found the Advantage of being train'd up in the Art of breaking our Battalions, which we were at this time very expert at; so that while the Horse were engaging each other, our Commanding Officers, according to the Manner I have describ'd, soon drew their Battalions out of this Confusion,

King William, *in* Ireland *and in* Flanders.

sion, and form'd them in Order, by which Time our Horse having routed those of the Enemy, we then prest in upon their Centre, who still maintain'd their Ground. But about this Time an accidental Cannon Shot having taken off St. *Ruth*'s Head, whereby their Army was at a great Loss for want of his Orders, especially Lieutenant-General *Sarsfield*, whom he had posted with a Body of Reserve in the Rear, with positive Directions not to stir from thence until he receiv'd his Orders; and tho' *Sarsfield* saw Opportunities of doing great Service, yet he would not stir, till he saw their whole Army put to the Route, when he was oblig'd to make off with the Crowd without striking a Stroke.

Thus ended the Battle of *Aughrim*, in which the greatest Part of the *Irish* Army behaved to Admiration; and had not St. *Ruth* been taken off, and had those in the Ditches done their Duty a little better, it would be hard to say what would have been the Consequence of that Day.

The Loss of the Enemy was computed to be about 17,000 kill'd and taken, with all their Camp and Baggage, and what Cannon they had.

Our Army had upwards of 4000 kill'd and wounded. We halted about a Mile from the Field of Battle, and next Day made the Prisoners bury the Dead; and the Day following our Tents and Baggage being come up, we march'd towards *Galway*, where was a Garrison of near 2000 poor sorry Fellows with hardly a Rag on their Backs, who surrender'd the third Day after we came before it, having Liberty to march to *Limerick*, whither the greatest Part of their shatter'd Troops had fled. Our General march'd in the greatest Haste to *Limerick*, where he found the Enemy had taken up the same Ground on *Tumond* Side the River, they had done the preceding

1691.

ceding Year, and for the Conveniency of being supplied with Necessaries, we were oblig'd to take up the Ground on the other Side; but our General soon found that *Limerick* was not to be taken in any reasonable Time, unless he could dislodge the Enemy, and so invest it round. Now the difficult Matter was, in passing the River upon them at this Place, for he could not quit the Ground he was on for the above Reason; and the Enemy being sensible of this, they kept strict Guards constantly patrolling by Night on the River Side, but drew out of the Reach of our Cannon by Day.

However, our General found Means to have a Correspondence with Col. *Lutterell*, who having a plentiful Fortune in the Kingdom, and loth to lose it, promis'd when he had the Guard of the River to give us an Opportunity of laying Bridges over it; and when the Night came that he had the Guard he gave us Notice, and order'd his Patroles a different Way from the Place where the Bridges were to be laid, so that we laid our Bridges, and pass'd Part of the Army before Day; and the Morning proving foggy we march'd up to the Enemy's Camp, and were the first that carried them the News of our Passing, which was such a Surprize to them, that the Foot, most of 'em naked, without making the least Resistance made away to the Town, where the Gates being shut against them, great Numbers were kill'd under the Walls, and also a great many of ours kill'd from the Walls, by their too eager Pursuit of them.

The Horse also fled half naked, most of them without Bridle or Saddle, away towards the farthest Part of the County of *Clare*; and now we invested *Limerick*, which brought on the Capitulation, by which they surrender'd both Town and Kingdom; which put an End to the Wars of *Ireland*.

King William, *in* Ireland *and in* Flanders.

In *May*, 23 Battalions (of which our Regiment 1692. was one) embark'd at *Waterford*, and landed at *Briſtol*; from whence we march'd to *Portſmouth*, where we imbark'd with a Deſign of making a Deſcent into *France*; but when we came to that Coaſt, we found it ſo ſtrongly guarded, that our General did not think proper to land, ſo we return'd to the *Downs*; where we lay until the King, who was then in *Flanders*, ſent Orders for us to ſail to *Oſtend*, where we landed; and march'd to *Furnes* and *Dixmude*. Upon our Approach to thoſe Places, the *French* quitted them; and after we had put them in a better State of Defence, the greateſt Part of our Troops march'd back to *Oſtend*, where we reimbark'd and return'd to *England*; but in our Paſſage met with a violent Tempeſt, in which ſome Ships periſh'd, however our Regiment got ſafe, and quarter'd this Winter in *Briſtol*.

In *May*, we march'd to *Portſmouth*, and em- 1693. bark'd with ſeveral other Regiments, on board the Grand Fleet, where we ſerv'd this Summer as Marines. The Fleet was commanded by three joint Admirals, Sir *Ralf De Lavel*, Sir *Cloudeſly Shovell*, and Admiral *Killegrew*, and Sir *George Rook* had a Squadron of twenty Men of War to convoy the *Smyrna* Fleet up the *Mediterranean*. Our Admirals had Orders to ſail with Sir *George* till they ſaw him paſt the *Bay* of *Biſcay*, and then return. The *French* had an Account of this, whereupon they order'd their Squadron at *Breſt*, and ſome Ships from *Toulon* to join at *Lagos-Bay*, in *Portugal*, and there wait for the Coming of Sir *George*. And ſuch was the Treachery of thoſe Times, that even ſome of our Admirals were ſuſpected to be in the Secret; when Sir *Cloudſley* preſt the other two to continue but Twenty-four Hours in that Latitude, they ſail'd on, till they heard
what

1693. what might happen to Sir *George*; yet, tho' they knew the *French* were waiting for him, they would not hearken, but sail'd immediately back.——Sir *George* being sensible of his Danger, kept a close Look-out; and upon spying the *French*, made a Signal for the Merchants to shift for themselves, while he kept in the Rear of them and made a runing Fight.

The *French* when they saw Sir *George*, did at first believe that our Grand Fleet had still kept him Company; whereupon they slipp'd their Cables, and were standing away for *Cadiz*, till an *Hamburgher* that had sail'd away from Sir *George* in the Night gave them an Account how Matters were, upon which they tack'd about, and made all the Sail they could after him; but Sir *George* by that Means having got so far a-head of them, that only a few light Sailors came up with him, who durst not come too near, so that he return'd safe, and but a few of the heavy Sailors of the Merchantmen were pick'd up by the Privateers. Our Troops landed in *September*, and our Regiment march'd to *Norwich*, where we lay about six Weeks, and then march'd to *London*, where we were review'd by the King in *Hyde-Park*, and two Days after embark'd at the *Red-House*, from whence we sail'd to *Ostend*, where we landed in *December*, and quarter'd until the Spring.

1694. We join'd the Army in *Flanders*. In *May* the King took the Field, and rendezvous'd the Army at *Bethlehem*, near *Louvain*, where he found the same compleat 90,000. From hence we march'd to *Rosebeck*, where a Dispute arose about the Rank of our Regiment in particular, which had regimented in King *Charles* the Second's Time out of the old Independent Companies in *Ireland*, and had hitherto taken Rank of all the Regiments rais'd by King *James*

the

the Second, but now thofe Regiments difputed the Rank with us; on which the King referr'd the Matter to a Board of General Officers, and moft of them being Colonels of thofe Regiments, would allow our Regiment no other Rank than from our firft coming into *England*, which was fometime before the King landed, when he came over Prince of *Orange* on the Revolution; by which we loft the Rank of eleven Regiments, fo we took Rank after all thofe rais'd by King *James*, and before all thofe rais'd by King *William*. The King himfelf thought the General Officers had acted with great Partiality, but as he had referred the Matter to them, fo he confirm'd it; and from hence it is, that all Regiments rais'd before (the Union) in *Ireland* and in *Scotland*, are to have no Rank in the Army until they enter upon the *Englifh* Eftablifhment.

The Duke of *Luxemberg* commanded the *French* Army, computed to be near 100,000, encamp'd near the Plains of *Mount St. Andrea*. The King advanc'd in order to give him Battle, but *Luxemberg* did not ftand it, but retired behind the *Main*, where there was no coming at him. We lay encamp'd on thefe Plains near fix Weeks; at length the King form'd a Scheme to get within the *French* Lines at *Point Efpiere*, in order to which he fent off the Elector of *Bavaria* with 20,000 Men, to march with all the Expedition he could to fecure that Pafs; at which Time he fent the heavy Baggage to *Bruffels*, and march'd the Army next Morning after the Elector; but this Affair could not be carried on fo fecretly but that *Luxemberg* had timely Notice of it; he fent off the Marfhal *Boufflers* with a ftrong Body of Horfe and Dragoons with Foot behind them, who got to the Pafs fometime before the Elector; and

18 MEMOIRS *of all the Campaigns of*

1694-5. *Luxemberg* with the reſt of the Army, march'd with what Expedition they could after him.

The King being diſappointed in this Affair, march'd lower down, paſs'd the *Scheld* near *Oudenard*, and encamp'd on the Plains near that Town, where we lay till our heavy Baggage came up, and then march'd to *Roſelare*, where we finiſh'd the Campaign. Our Regiment had *Ghent* for its Quarters, where we lay every Winter during this War.

This proving a Campaign of Action, I ſhall be more particular.

1695. The King having form'd a Deſign of beſieging *Namur*, took the Field the latter End of *April*, and encamp'd with the main Body of the Army between *Mennin* and *Ipris*, and made a Show as though he deſign'd to attack Fort *Knock*, while the Elector of *Bavaria* and the Earl of *Athlone* (General *Ginkell*) form'd a flying Camp near *Bruſſels*, under Pretence of covering that Part of the Country. The Duke *de Villeroy* commanded the *French* Army (*Luxemberg* being dead) who drew the main Body of his Army towards the King, and encamp'd within his Lines near *Mennin*, while *Boufflers*, with a flying Camp to obſerve the Motions of the Elector encamp'd near *Mons*; however, the Elector found Means to inveſt *Namur*, but could not prevent *Boufflers* from throwing himſelf with a good Body of Troops into it.

As ſoon as the King had an Account that *Namur* was inveſted, he immediately decamp'd, and after he had order'd Major-General *Ellinburg* to march with nine *Britiſh* Battalions, and a Regiment of Dragoons to *Dixmude*, to cover that Part of the Country, he left about 20,000 Men with Prince *Vademont*, to cover the Country about *Gaunt* and *Bruges*, and with the reſt of the Army he made what Haſte he could to *Namur*. Our Regiment was left there with the

Prince,

King William, *in* Ireland *and in* Flanders.

Prince, who took up the strong Camp of *Arsiel*, and caus'd a strong Intrenchment to be thrown up in the Front of his Camp.

Villeroy was not a little surpriz'd when he found *Namur* invested; however, was pleas'd when he heard that *Boufflers* had thrown himself into it with so good a Body of Troops; it being at this Time thought to be one of the strongest Places in *Europe*, and having in it a Marshal of *France*, the Marquis *De Guiscard*, Governor, an experienc'd Officer, with a Garrison of 14,000 Men, well provided with all Manner of Necessaries. Wherefore, before he would attempt raising the Siege, he try'd what he could do in these Parts; especially if he could but demolish *Vademont*, the Siege must rise in Course; whereupon as the King march'd off, *Villeroy* drew out of his Lines, and advanc'd with an Army of 90,000 Men towards *Vademont*; but finding him stand his Ground, he proceeded with the more Caution, and halted about two Leagues short of him, till he had sent to *Lisle* for some Battering Cannon. This took up some Time, which was what *Vademont* wanted, to keep him in Play till the King could fix himself before *Namur*. At Length *Villeroy* advanc'd within less than half a League of us, and finding the Prince still keep his Ground, order'd a great many Fascines to be cut in order to attack us early next Morning. He also sent Lieutenant-General *Montill* with a strong Body of Horse round by our Right, to fall in our Rear, and cut off our Retreat from *Gaunt*, which was three Leagues in the Rear of us. Now the Prince had three Capuchin Fryars for his Spies, one of whom kept constantly about *Villeroy*'s Quarters, who found Means to inform himself of all his Designs; the other two ply'd constantly between both Camps without ever being suspected, who gave *Vademont* an

Account of every Thing.———And now the Prince having drawn *Villeroy* so near him, he thought it high Time to make his Retreat; he therefore as soon as *Villeroy* appear'd, sent off all the heavy Baggage and Lumber of the Camp to *Gaunt*, and about Eight in the Evening, he order'd Part of the Cavalry to dismount and take the Intrenchments, and the Infantry to march privately off with their Pikes and Colours under-hand, left the Enemy should discover us drawing off; and as soon as it grew duskish the Cavalry mounted and march'd after the Foot. Soon after *Villeroy*'s Advance-Guard finding Matters very quiet in our Works, ventur'd upon them; who finding the Birds fled, sent to acquaint the General; on which they march'd after us as fast as they could. *Montill*, who by this Time had got into our Rear, finding us marching off, thought to have fallen on our Flank; but Sir *David Collier*, with two Brigades, gave them such a warm Reception, that oblig'd him to retire with considerable Loss. Next Morning all our Army was got safe under the Works of *Gaunt*, at which Time the Enemy's Horse began to appear within a Mile of us; whereupon we past the Canal that runs from this to *Bruges*, along which a Breast-Work had been thrown up. Thus have I given the best Account I can of this famous Retreat, in which both Generals were very much blam'd; *Villeroy* for not attacking us as soon as he came up, who with such a numerous Army might have over-run us with Ease; and *Vademont* for standing his Ground so long, and suffering Matters to be brought to such a Crisis; for one Day's Time would have signify'd but little in the Main. But what he had to say for himself, was, the Dependence he had on his Intelligence; which indeed by what follow'd, shews he had sufficient Reason to trust them; for he had now a very difficult Part to act

King William, *in* Ireland *and in* Flanders. 21

act in Defence of this Canal, against so powerful 1695.
an Army. *Villeroy* march'd immediately down to
the Canal, where, for upwards of three Weeks, by
Marchings and Countermarchings, he harrass'd our
small Army off their Legs; however, he could not
make the least Movement, or form any Design, but
the Prince had timely Notice of it, and it was very
strange he could have such Intelligence, considering
the Canal that was between us, so that the *French*
said he dealt with the Devil. *Villeroy* finding he
could not pass the Canal on the Prince, at Length
turn'd towards *Dixmude*, where the Prince could
give no Manner of Assistance.

Here Major-General *Ellinburg*, a *Dane*, who by his
personal Courage and Merit had rais'd himself from a private Centinel to be a Major-General in the *Danish* Service, and was particularly recommended to the King by
the Duke of *Wirtemberg*, who commanded the *Danish*
Forces, as a gallant experienc'd Officer for that Command, by his Behaviour here surpriz'd all that had ever
known him; for as soon as *Villeroy* appear'd, he call'd
all the commanding Officers together, and propos'd
sending to *Villeroy* to capitulate; to which they all
agreed, except the Commander of the Dragoons,
who exclaim'd heavily against it. However, he being
but one, an Officer was forthwith sent out to *Villeroy*,
to demand a Capitulation, who little expected so sudden a Message; he thereupon told the Officer, he would
allow them no other Terms than that of Prisoners of
War, and withall let them know, if they fir'd one Shot
at him he would put every Soul of them to the Sword;
and as soon as the Officer left him, he advanc'd with
the Army, and at once fell to breaking Ground.
Ellinburg, having before the Officer went out, given
Orders that not a Gun should be fir'd, upon the Return of the Officer they basely surrender'd on those

scandalous

1695. scandalous Terms. 'Tis true, the Fortifications were but indifferent; however such a noble Body of Troops, well provided as they were, might very well have held it out till a Lodgment had been made in the Counterscarp, which they could not have done in less than eight or ten Days; after which they might have been sure of having, at least as good, if not better Terms.

Thus was *Dixmude* surrender'd, and *Villeroy*, contrary to a Cartel which had been agreed upon but the Winter before for the Release of Prisoners, sent them all away, and dispers'd both Officers and Soldiers throughout the Kingdom of *France*. From *Dixmude Villeroy* march'd to *Deinse*, into which Place *Vademont*, upon his Retreat from *Arsiel*, had order'd Brigadier *Offarel* with two Battalions; who upon the Arrival of *Villeroy*, surrender'd after the same Manner as *Dixmude*.

Villeroy having loiter'd away a great deal of Time in these Parts, was now for drawing towards *Namur*, but resolv'd on taking *Brussels* in his Way, proposing to give the Sackage of that famous City to his Soldiers; but *Vademont*, whose Intelligence never fail'd him, had timely Notice, and got thither before him, and posted his Army in such a Manner as prevented his taking the Town, but could not hinder him from bombarding it; by which he laid a great Part of it in Ashes.

Villeroy thought it high Time to march to the Relief of *Namur*, the Siege of which Place being far advanced; for the King had oblig'd *Boufflers* to deliver up the Town on the 4th of *July*, who retir'd with his Troops into the Castle; against which his Majesty was carrying on the most vigorous Siege, and battering it with 160 Battering Cannon, and 50 Mortars.

It

King William, *in* Ireland *and in* Flanders.

It was now the 4th of *August* when *Villeroy* drew 1695. off from *Bruſſels*. He firſt march'd to the Plains of *Fleury*, where he ſtaid till he was reinforc'd from all the Garriſons thereabouts, which compleated to more than 100,000. Upon his marching from *Bruſſels*, *Vademont* march'd and join'd the King, who lay with the Covering Army behind the *Mehaigne*, near two Leagues from *Namur*, and about a League behind him was his Circumvallation Line. The Elector of *Bavaria* carried on the Siege with 20,000 Men.

The very next Day after we join'd the King, being the 12th of *August*, four of our *Britiſh* Battalions that were with the Prince, were ordered to the Siege, (of which ours was one) where we arriv'd Time enough to come in for our Share of it. On the 16th *Villeroy* advanc'd towards the King, and encamp'd within a League of him: Next Day he march'd and drew up in Line of Battle within Cannon-Shot of him, where they ſtaid ſome Hours, while *Villeroy* was taking a View of the King's Situation; which it ſeems he did by no Means like, wherefore he march'd back to his Camp, and two Days after he made ſuch another Motion, and plainly ſaw there was no Poſſibility of forcing the King's Camp, without running the Riſque of his whole Army.——
While *Villeroy* was thus amuſing the King, a general Aſſault was order'd to be made, for making a Lodgment on the Covert-way of the Caſtle.——
The Evening before this famous Attack, there came from the King's Camp a Detachment of 2000 Grenadiers and 5000 Fuziliers, who march'd into the Trenches as ſoon as they arriv'd, and the next Morning before Day moſt of the beſieging Army march'd alſo into the Trenches, but were ſo crouded, that our Regiment, with one more, were oblig'd to draw up within the Walls of *Salſine-Abbey*, which was near

half

1695. half an *English* Mile from the Place where we were to make our Attack.

August 20, O. S. About Ten o'Clock in the Forenoon the Signal was given, at which time the Lord *Cutts*, at the Head of the *British* Grenadiers, supported by our four *British* Battalions, attack'd the Breach that was made by the *Terra Nova*; the *Bavarians* attack'd the Cohorn (where the Elector was present.) The *Dutch* attack'd the Works about the *Devil's Knees*, under the Direction of the Duke of *Holstein-Ploen*; and the Works from thence to the *Maze* were attack'd by the *Brandenburgers*, *Hanoverians* and *Hessians*, under the Direction of Prince *Nassau Sarbruck*.

The Lord *Cutts*, with the Grenadiers, were beat off before they got half-way up the Breach, as were also two of the Battalions; but our Regiment, and the others that were within the Walls of *Salsine*-Abbey, having a greater Distance, could not come up to the Breach till they were beat off; however, we mounted the very Top of it: but by Reason of a strange Retrenchment which the Enemy had thrown up on the Inside, we could proceed no farther; so we were obliged to retire, and make the best of our Way back.

This was the only Breach made in all their Works; nor could a Lodgment be made there for the high Work of the *Terra Nova*.

The *Bavarians*, and all the other Attacks made the Lodgment they design'd on the Covert-Way, which answer'd the Design of the Attack.

The Loss the Allies sustain'd on this Occasion was very considerable; which in some measure might be computed by the Loss of our Regiment in particular, but do believe we were the greatest Sufferers of any. We had kill'd our Lieut. Colonel, four Captains, and seven

seven Subalterns; the wounded were our Colonel, three Captains, and 10 Subalterns, with 271 private Men kill'd and wounded.

The King beheld this Action from a rising Ground on the Back of the *Salsine*-Abbey, from whence he took particular Notice of the Behaviour of our Regiment, when he saw us alone mount the Top of the Breach, and plant our Colours thereon, for which his Majesty was pleased the Winter following to honour the Regiment with the Title of ROYAL of IRELAND, and gave Commissions accordingly.

This Attack being over, *Boufflers* plainly saw, by the Lodgments that had been made, that another would soon follow, which might be of fatal Consequence to himself and Garrison; he therefore early next Morning made Signals of Distress from the Top of the Castle, which *Villeroy* easily perceiv'd; and finding it impossible to relieve him, next Morning being the 22d, he set Fire to his Camp, and march'd off, which was a Signal to *Boufflers* to make the best Terms he could for himself; whereupon *Boufflers* the same Day beat the Chamade, upon which Hostages were exchanged, and a Capitulation entered upon. *Boufflers* would fain excuse himself from treating, but was for putting it upon the Governor, as thinking it beneath a Marshal of *France* to treat of a Surrender; but the King would by no Means allow of it, nor would the Governor take it upon him: so the Elector and *Boufflers* carried on the Capitulation, which was agreed upon as follows; That on the 26th the Garrison should march out with Drums beating, Colours flying, six Pieces of Cannon, as many cover'd Waggons, with some other Marks of Honour. According to this Capitulation, *Boufflers* and the Governor marched out at the Head of their Troops, consisting of 8000. Our Troops made a Lane for them to march thro'; as soon as they had got clear of the Castle, *Mynheer Duckvelt*, one of the Field-Deputies of the States General went up to *Boufflers*, and desir'd to speak with him by himself; to which *Boufflers* readily comply'd, believing he had something of Consequence to communicate to him; but was very much surprized when he found himself surrounded by a Body of Horse, and told he was the King of *England*'s Prisoner, who had order'd him to be arrested on account of the Garrisons of *Dixmude* and *Deinse*, who were detained contrary to the Capitulation that had been agreed on for the Release of Prisoners.

Boufflers in a mighty Rage desir'd he might send to the Elector of *Bavaria*, with whom he had made his Capitulation, the which was granted him; to whom he complain'd of the Violation of his Treaty, and let him know, that the King his Master would not fail revenging the Affront. The Elector, in Answer, let him know, that the King of *England* commanded, and that he made use of this Expedient to prevent the perpetual Infractions which his Master generally made on all Cartels and Capitulations, contrary to the Law of Arms; whereupon he was forced to submit, and was sent Prisoner to *Mastricht*, where he remained till those Troops were ordered back. Soon after the Surrender of the Castle of *Namur*, the King drew into the Field, and offered *Villeroy* Battle, but he declin'd it, and march'd within his Lines: so nothing was done this Campaign, both Armies going early into Quarters, and soon after the Garrisons of *Dixmude* and *Deinse* were returned, upon which the King order'd a general Court Martial to be held at *Gaunt*, for trying the Commanding Officers of those Garrisons.

Major-General *Ellinburg* said but little in his Defence, but frankly own'd, from the very Moment he
received

King William, *in* Ireland *and in* Flanders.

received Orders for that Command, a Pannick seized 1695. him, which he could not get over, nor account for.

The Commanding Officers of the Regiments urged in their Defence, that, as they were under the Command of the Major-General, they thought themselves obliged to obey. This Pretence had but little Weight with the Court Martial, as appears by their Sentence, which was, that Major-General *Ellinburg* should have his Head cut off by the common Executioner of the *Danish* Forces; and all the Commanding Officers that signed the Capitulation should be broke, and rendred incapable of ever serving the Crown of *England* more; but they recommended the Commanding Officer of the Dragoons to his Majesty for Preferment.

Brigadier *Offarrel* a Man of long Service, who had always behaved well, had something to say for himself, *viz.* That *Deinse* was but a poor fortified Village, hardly sufficient to keep out a Partizan Party; and the slender Garrison he had in it was not sufficient to defend it from so numerous an Army running over the Works of it, without so much as firing a Gun against it.

The Commanding Officers alledg'd the same, however the Court Martial passed Sentence, purely to set an Example to others; that the Brigadier should be cashier'd the Service, and rendred incapable of serving the Crown of *England* more, and the Commanding Officer to be suspended for four Months, and then restored.

Their great Crime was in not making some Shew of Resistance, and firing some Cannon at them; nor was it expected that they should stand a general Assault, for the Design of throwing Troops into those Places was only to keep the Enemy employ'd as long as they could: and it was never known, that an Enemy, tho' ever so well provided, or assured of Suc-

cess

cess on any Attack, did refuse a Capitulation when offered; an Instance of this we had this very Campaign: Capt. *Withers* of Col. *Calthorp*'s Regiment being posted in a *Chateau* with only six Men, stood against *Villeroy*'s whole Army for some Hours; and when he saw they were preparing to storm him, he then beat the Chamade, on which he had the same Terms granted him, and himself and Men better treated than those that surrendred without firing a Shot: which may be a sufficient Instance to all Officers, in regard to their Honour, and the Good of the Service, that they be not too forward in delivering up Places committed to their Charge; nor yet too fool-hardy in standing out till an Attack is once begun: for then it will be too late, I mean the attacking a Breach, or such Works as may be easily carry'd; especially when there is not a considerable Force to oppose.

The King confirm'd the Sentence of the Court Martial, and every thing was executed accordingly.

1696. Notwithstanding that the King had out-brav'd the Enemy the two former Campaigns, he was now obliged to act on the Defensive; for the *French* King having clapp'd up a Peace with the Duke of *Savoy* last Winter, it enabled him to send a greater Number of Troops to the *Netherlands*, than he had any time before; and his Majesty's great Disappointments at home from a perverse Sett of Men, who had continued a Conspiracy for assassinating him, was now so streightned for Money, on account of calling in the old Coin, that he had not wherewithal to pay the Army; nor could he take the Field a Fortnight after the Enemy: However he made a Shift to prevent them from getting any Advantage.

Villeroy encamp'd with the main Body of his Army on the Plain of *Cambroon*, and *Boufflers* with the remaining Part near *Roselaire*.

King William, *in* Ireland *and in* Flanders.

The King, with the Elector of *Bavaria*, encamp'd 1696. with the Grofs of his Army at *Hall*, to cover *Bruffels*, and that Part of the Country; and Prince *Vademont*, with the remaining Part, encamp'd along the Canal betwixt *Gaunt* and *Bruges*.

Both Armies lay all this Campaign looking at one another, without one Attempt, which feem'd as tho' all Parties grew weary of this long expenfive War; fo both Armies broke up, and went early to Quarters; and foon after a Treaty was fet on foot at *Ryfwick* in *Holland*.

In *May* both Armies took the Field.

The *French* King, to make a pompous Show in 1697. the *Netherlands* in this laft Campaign of the War, fent Marfhal *Catinate* with more Troops to join *Villeroy* and *Boufflers*, in fo much that the Army was prodigioufly increas'd.

Thefe three Marfhals drew their Army together on the Plains of *Cambroon*, and were almoft double our Number.

The King, who encamp'd at *Bois-fenior Iffaau*, was obliged to have a watchful Eye over the Enemy; about the Middle of *June* they decamp'd and advanc'd towards us, upon which the King decamp'd and march'd towards *Promel*; but finding the Enemies Defign was upon *Bruffels*, he turn'd that Way, and by continuing our March all Night, got thither fome Hours before them, and took up the ftrong Camp of *Anderleck*, where we fell immediately to work in throwing up a ftrong Intrenchment with Redoubts, and other ftrong Works, which effectually fecur'd both the Town and Army.

This Security of *Bruffels* was a very important Affair at this Juncture; for had the Enemy got thither before us, it would have had a mighty Effect in the Treaty of *Ryfwick*, which was now almoft brought

to

1696. to a Close. The Enemy finding we had secur'd *Brussels*, stop'd short at *Hall*, and sent a Detachment from thence to lay Siege to *Aeth*; and tho' they knew the Peace would be concluded by the Time *Aeth* would be taken, and that in Course it must be delivered back, yet such was the Vanity of the haughty Monarch of *France*, that this he would do, to let the World see (as he boasted) it was out of his own Generosity he gave Peace to *Europe*.

By the Time *Aeth* was taken, the Congress at *Ryswick* had concluded on all Matters, except some few Things relating to King *James*, which were settled in Camp between the Earl of *Portland* and the Marshal *Boufflers*, and so put an End to this long and bloody War.

In *September* both Armies quitted the Field, at which the Allies separated and returned to their respective Countries; our *British* Troops lay in *Ghent* and *Bruges*, until Shipping arrived at *Ostend* for carrying us off.

Our Regiment, with the Troops for *Ireland*, sail'd in *December*, where we continued till the breaking out of the next War, which will be the Subject of the Second Part of my Memoirs.

Queen ANNE's *Wars*.

1700. In 1700 died *Charles* King of *Spain*, who had been languishing many Years, on whose Death *Lewis* XIV. broke through all the sacred Ties of the late Peace, to place his Grandson *Philip* on that Throne, contrary to the express Articles of the said Treaty, and had brought over to his Interest the two Electors of *Bavaria* and *Cologne*.

The first being Governour of the *Spanish Netherlands*, delivered to him all the Garrisons of those Coun-

of the Duke of Marlborough.   31

Countries that belonged to *Spain*; and the latter all 1701-2.
the Garrisons that belong'd to his Electorate. Whereupon King *William* form'd another Grand Alliance against this ambitious Monarch, on which a fresh War commenced.

In 1701 the *British* Troops were ordered to *Holland*, at which Time our Regiment with eleven others sailed from *Cork*, and in the Beginning of *July* arrived in the *Maese*, from whence we were dispers'd into Quarters.

1702. The first Thing the Allies undertook this War in the *Netherlands*, was the Siege of *Keyserswaert*, a strong Town on the other side the *Rhine*, which belongs to the Electorate of *Cologn*, but garrisoned by *France*.

The Allies form'd the Siege of this Place in *April*, on which the *French* King sent above 60000 Men, under the Duke of *Burgundy*, and the Marshal *Boufflers*, in order to raise the Siege.

On the Arrival of the *French* Army, the Earl of *Athlone* formed a Camp of about 20000 Men, at *Cranenburg*, three Leagues from *Nimeguen*, and two from *Cleves*, in order to cover that Part of the Country, while the Siege was carrying on; in this Camp were most of the *British* Troops.

The Enemy lay encamped about five Leagues in our Front, between whom was a large thick Wood, not passable for an Army; they lay on the opposite Side of the *Rhine* to *Keyserswart*, but durst not attempt passing the River on the Allies; so all they could do, was to send fresh Troops in Boats over the River by Night, to bring back their wounded.

This enabled the Garrison to hold out some time longer; but when *Burgundy* found that he could not prevent the Allies from taking it, he formed a Scheme to fall on our small Army under *Athlone*; in order

1702. to which, as they were beating Tattoo, they decamped on a sudden. The Duke of *Burgundy* with the right Wing taking his Front round the Wood, by the Way of *Cleves*, and *Boufflers* with the Left, round by the Way of *Gennefp*. My Lord *Athlone* had no Account of the March of the Enemy, 'till twelve o' clock next Day, when on a sudden he gave Orders to strike our Tents, and to march. These Orders gave us no small Alarm, especially those who had sent their Horses this Morning to *Nimeguen* for Forage, which was the Case of our Regiment for one; so we march'd, leaving our Tents and Baggage on the Ground behind us, never expecting to see them more: However, Expresses were sent for the Horses to throw away their Forage, and make what Haste they could to bring off the Tents and Baggage, which they very luckily effected.

We continued our March all the Night, but were obliged to take something of a Round to leave the great Road for the Artillery and Baggage; at which Time the Enemies Horse began to appear on both sides of us, but their Infantry was a good Distance behind; this made us quicken our March, yet before we could reach the Town, a Party of their Dragoons made a Push at some of our Infantry, which put them in Disorder; but the Dragoons were soon obliged to retreat, and we got safe within the Out-works of *Nimeguen*. My Lord *Athlone*, at the Head of the Cavalry, kept in Rear of the Foot, and behaved with great Bravery, but was much blamed for not having better Intelligence; half an Hour more would have brought their Infantry, which would have done our Business; the Artillery and Baggage having the short Cut, got safe.

This small Army narrowly escap'd being cut to Pieces for want of good Intelligence, which shews the
Necessity

of the Duke of Marlborough.

Necessity a General lies under to keep a number of trusty Spies.

1702.

Soon after this Retreat *Keyserswaert* surrendered, and the Army joined near *Nimeguen*, where the Earl of *Marlbro'* came and took upon him the Command of the Army in the *Netherlands*, which he found compleat 70000 Men. Soon after his coming, he advanced towards the Enemy, who had taken up the strong Camp of *Gennep*, with their Left close to the *Maese*.

My Lord *Marlboro'* knew that the Eyes of all the Confederates were upon him, he never having had the like Command before; but especially the States General, who purely to oblige the Queen of *England*, not only placed him at the Head of their Army, but even the Safety of their Country in a great Measure depended upon his Conduct: However, as it had always been the Practice of that wise State, even in the King's Time, to send two of their Council of State with Generals into the Field, who always acted in Concert, they sent with my Lord two of the most experienced Men amongst them as their Field Deputies, which my Lord could not take ill, since it had been their constant Practice, tho', as he ever after did, watched all Opportunities to give a bold Stroke at his first setting out to fix a Reputation.

The first Thing the States wanted, was to clear the *Maese* of all the *French* Garrisons between *Holland* and *Maestricht*, which the Enemy knew, and posted themselves in the Way. My Lord *Marlboro'* finding there was no attacking them in the Camp they were in, form'd a Scheme to draw the Enemy after him.

Our Army lay encamped within two Leagues of them, with our Right close to the *Maese*, over which

1702. which my Lord order'd Bridges to be laid, under Pretence of supplying the Camp with Forage from the other Side of the River; as soon as the Bridges were finished he made a grand Forage, which looked as if he designed to continue for some time in this Camp; but the next Evening, on beating the Tattoo, Orders came to strike our Tents to march, whereupon we pass'd the River, and continued marching all that Night, and till Noon next Day, at which Time we came up with the Castle of *Gravenbrook*, in which were three hundred of the Enemy, who refusing to surrender at Discretion, stood it out about four Hours, till the Castle Works were beat about their Ears, and then surrendered, and had the same Terms as first offered. Here the Governor behaved like a Man of Honour and true Judgment; for he would not surrender till he was attacked, nor was so rash as to stand an Assault. From hence we continued our March the same Evening, to *Hubert's-Hill*, where we pitch'd our Camp.

The Enemy were surprized when they found my Lord had given them the Slip; but were much more so, when they found he had got between them and home; whereupon they decamped, and marched along the River till they came within two Leagues of *Vinte*, and then passed it, and encamped within three Leagues of the Left of our Army; and were in great Perplexity to get by us.

Marshal *Tallard* at this Time had a flying Camp of about 12 or 14000 Men in these Parts, to take Care of their Lines, to whom the Duke of *Burgundy* sent to advance towards us, to favour his Attempt.

Our Army had at a little Distance in Front a large Heath, over which the Enemy could not avoid passing. The Enemy halted in their Camp.

The Day after they had paſſed the River, and the Morning following they made a grand Forage, as if they deſign'd to make ſome Stay; but my Lord knew very well it was no Camp for them to dwell in; and that That Forage was a Feint to get by him next Morning: He thereupon ordered the Army to ſtrike their Tents, and ſend them with all the Baggage away to *Gravenbrook*, and lie on our Arms all Night, to be ready to fall on the Enemy in the Morning, as they paſſed the Heath. As my Lord judged, it happened; for upon the Enemies beating the Tattoo, they ſtruck their Camp, and marched with all poſſible Expedition, and were entering the Heath by Dawn; at which Time my Lord had the Army under Arms, and ready to march, when the Field Deputies came and pray'd him to deſiſt, notwithſtanding they had the Evening before conſented. My Lord was very much chagrin'd at this Diſappointment; for, in all human Probability, we ſhould have given the Enemy a fatal Blow; ſo my Lord not being willing to do any Thing this firſt Campaign without their Approbation, with great Reluctance complied, and returned with the Army; however he deſired they would ride out with him to ſee the Enemy paſs the Heath, which they did, and were ſurprized to ſee their great Hurry and Confuſion, and confeſs'd a great Opportunity was loſt by their Means. When an Army is under ſuch a Conſternation as the *French* were at this Time, 'tis not to be imagined what a ſmall Matter puts all into Confuſion. Thus they had a narrow Eſcape of being cut to Pieces; 'tis true *Tallard* appeared at a Diſtance, which was the only Motive that induced the Field Deputies againſt engaging; nor could they tell how my Lord *Marlbro'* might behave when he came to engage.

1072.

Burgundy

Burgundy and *Tallard* being now joined, their Army out-numbered ours by eight or ten thousand Men, notwithstanding my Lord was for giving them Battle; but he found both they and the Field Deputies were for avoiding it.

Next Day my Lord made a Movement with the Army to front the Enemy, where he was obliged to halt for the coming up of our Bread-Waggons and Pay-Masters, that were waiting at the *Graave* for a Convoy to bring them up; whereupon he made a Detachment of 1600 Men under the Command of General *Opdam* for that Purpose; there was an *English* Brigadier in this Detachment, in which was our Regiment, commanded by Lord *Cutts*. Upon *Opdam*'s marching off, the *French* made a Movement that Way, with a Design of falling on him. My Lord was in Hopes this might bring on a general Engagement, whereupon he marched after *Opdam*, keeping at such a Distance that he might be ready to succour him in Case he should be attacked, on which the *French* halted, who all this Time kept within the inclosed Part of the Country, but my Lord kept out in the open Plains; at last *Opdam* brought up the Convoy within a League of my Lord's Camp, at which Time my Lord finding the Enemy had still their Eye on the Convoy, he marched the Army away towards *Peer* and *Dunderslaugh* Heath, ordering *Opdam* to follow him; by which he was in Hopes of drawing the Enemy into this large Heath. This Bait the Enemy took; for finding my Lord marching on, they came out of the inclosed Grounds with a Design of falling on the Convoy; but my Lord kept a watchful Eye on them, and rightly judging the Part of the Heath they would come to, he stopt short with the Army, and edged back towards *Opdam*. By this Time the Enemy were drawn so far

into

into the Heath, that they could not get back without great Danger of having part of their Army cut off; they therefore put on the best Face, and drew up in Order of Battle; *Opdam* drew up his Detachment on the Right of the Army, and the Convoy with all the Baggage fell in the Rear.

Both Armies were drawn up on a noble Heath, within half a Mile of each other, so that it was thought impossible we could part without Blows; the Cannon on both sides play'd with great Fury, whereby many Men were killed. About five o'clock my Lord *Marlbro'* having put every thing in Order, was just on beginning the Battle when the Field Deputies, who were insensibly, as well as the Enemy, brought into this Scrape, came to him, and desired him not to engage until Morning, that he might have the Day before him; but my Lord told them, the Enemy would not stay till the Morning; however, on their pressing Importunities he did forbear; and, just as he said, next Morning there was not one of them to be seen, but some few of their Squadrons at great Distance, bringing up their Rear, and never halted till they had got within their Lines. After this my Lord set about clearing the *Maese* of the *French* Garrisons; in order to which *Opdam* was sent off with his Detachment to lay Siege to *Venlo*, and my Lord marched with the rest of the Army, and encamp'd near *Maestricht*, where he lay to cover the besieging Army.

It was on the 16th of *August* when *Opdam* came before *Venlo*. We encamped on the West side of the River, and carried on our Approaches against Fort *St. Michael*, that lay on our Side of the Water. The second Day after our Arrival Prince *Nassau Sarbrook* arrived on the other Side the River with about 18000 *Prussians*, *Hanoverians* and *Hessians*, who

1702. carried on their Approaches againſt the Town, which lay altogether on that Side.

We carried on our Approaches againſt Fort *St. Michael* by three Attacks; an *Engliſh* Brigade had one of them; theſe Approaches were ſoon carried to the Foot of the Glacis, on which Orders were given to make a Lodgment for attacking the Covert Way, to join our three Attacks by a Parallel Line.

As there happen'd an Affair upon this Occaſion, in which our whole Regiment was concerned, I ſhall be the more particular in my Relation.

Our Regiment mounted the Trenches of our Attack the Morning before this Attack was made; about Noon there joined us the three Companies of Grenadiers that were of our Attack, with five hundred Fuſiliers. About two o'clock the Lord *Cutts*, with ſeveral young Noblemen, came into the Trenches to ſee the Attack carried on. A little before the Attack began, my Lord *Cutts* called the Officers together, and told us, that if we found the Enemy give way with Precipitation, then we were to jump into their Works, follow them, let the Conſequence be what it would. Theſe were fine Orders from a General; but as inconſiderate as they were, we as inconſiderately and raſhly followed them.

About four o'clock the Signal was given; on our advancing, the Enemy gave us their fire and run; we jump'd into the Covert-Way, and purſued; they made to a Ravelin which cover'd the Curtain of the Fort, and a ſmall wooden Bridge which was over a Fauſſee, by which they reliev'd their outward Works; we drove them into the Ravelin, where was a Captain and ſixty Men; we ſoon diſpatch'd moſt of them, the reſt fled over the Bridge, and we, Madmen-like, followed till we got on the Fauſſee-bray, under the Body of the Fort; the Port being ſhut,

shut, those that fled before us climb'd it up, which 1702. shew'd us the Way; for we had no Choice, but to carry the Fort or all perish; we climbed after them: The Enemy were confounded, and made but little Resistance, soon quitted the Rampart, and retired into the Body of the Fort, where they threw down their Arms and called for Quarters, which we gave them, and the Plunder of the Fort to the Soldiers. Thus were the Lord *Cutts*'s unaccountable Orders as unaccountably executed; but had not several unexpected Accidents occur'd in the Affair, hardly a Man of us would have escaped being either killed, drowned, or taken.

As first, the Ditch round the Ravelin was dry, and their own Men shew'd us the Way into it; then the unexpected Bridge which led over the Moat, where there was Planks for those of the Ravelin to have drawn after them when they found themselves attack'd, which the Capt. of the Ravelin should have done, when he saw us coming in so furious a Manner; so that had those Planks been drawn over to their Side, we must have made a full Stop here, and the Foremost, in Course, must have been thrust into the Moat by those that came after, where they must have perish'd, there being eight or ten Feet of Water, and upwards of one hundred Feet over; and again, when we had got over on the Fauffee-bray, had there been but eight or ten Feet of Brick or Stone-Work under the Sod, as is now practis'd in all Modern Fortifications, we could never have climb'd as we did, nor even as it was, had not the Grass been long enough for us to hold by; and it may be easily judged what the Consequence must have been: But the Success of the Affair crown'd the Event, which got the Lord *Cutts* great Applause, of which he boasted all his Life after, tho' neither he nor any of the Noblemen stir'd one Foot out of the Trenches till we were Masters of it, except the young Earl of *Huntington*, who stole out of the Trenches from them, and kept up with the foremost.

Another remarkable Affair happened on the Surrender of the Town, *viz.* An Account came to the Prince, that the *Germans* had taken *Landau*, on which he ordered the Army on both sides the River, to draw down as near to the Town as they could conveniently to fire; for that Purpose, when the Garrison and Inhabitants saw the Army drawing down on all sides of them, they were strangely surprized, believing it was with a Design of making such another Attack on the Town, as had been made on the Fort but two Days before: Whereupon the Garrison got all to their Arms, the Magistrates run away to the Governour, begging him to capitulate, and not suffer them all to fall a Sacrifice to the Fury of the Enemy. The Inhabitants also, Men, Women and Children, came flocking to the Ramparts with white Cloths in their Hands, crying out Mercy, Mercy, Quarter, Quarter. The Governor himself was under no less Consternation than the Inhabitants, he dispatch'd an Officer to desire a Capitulation; the Prince upon this Message was as much surprized as any, and sent immediately to stop our firing, being then in the middle of our second Round, whereupon a Capitulation ensued; and as there were several Garrisons more on the River to be taken this Campaign, so the Prince granted them upon honourable Terms, and the second Day after the Garrison marched out; and the Day following *Opdam* passed the *Maese*, and join'd the Prince, and then marched to *Ruremond*, to which we laid Siege, and took it in about two Weeks.

While

of the Duke of Marlborough.

While we were carrying on this Siege, my Lord Marlbro' sent a Detachment from the Grand Army, which took in *Stephenswert* and *Mazewich*, by which the *Maese* was clear'd of the *French* Garrisons up to *Maestricht*.

After this the whole Army join'd on *Petersbourg*, a League above *Maestricht*, from whence we march'd to *Liege*, where Marshal *Boufflers* was encamped with the *French* Army, in Hopes to prevent that City's falling to the Allies; but on our Approach he retired within his Lines, leaving eleven Battalions in the Citadel, and two in the Chartreuse.

The Magistrates brought the Keys of the City to my Lord, and received a Garrison; the Siege of the Citadel was carried on altogether on the Outside of the Town; and by the 12th of *October* a considerable Breach being made, we storm'd and carried it Sword in Hand. The Chartreuse being an Eyewitness of the Fate of the Citadel, surrendered on Summons, which ended my Lord *Marlbro*'s first Campaign.

The *British* Troops were ordered to their former Quarters in *Holland*; and when Matters were settled for quartering the Troops, my Lord *Marlbro'* went down the *Maese* in a Yacht with the Field Deputies; but when he had got below *Venlo*, a *French* Partizan Party from *Guelders* seiz'd the Horses that drew the Yacht, and made them all Prisoners; but the Field Deputies producing the Duke of *Burgundy*'s Pass, and making them a handsome Present, which was what they wanted more than Prisoners, and not knowing my Lord, after rifling the Yacht of some valuable Things, they let them pass, and they got safe to the *Hague*.

The Queen having last Winter created the Earl Duke of *Marlborough*, he came early in this Spring, and

1702.

1703.

1703. and after he had settled Matters with the *States* about the Campaign, he gave Orders for the *British* and *Dutch* Troops to assemble near *Maſtricht*, under the Command of the Veldt-Marſhal *Auverquerque*, whilſt he with the *Pruſſian, Hanoverian*, and *Heſſian* Troops undertook the Siege of *Bonn*, which he obliged to ſurrender in leſs than three Weeks; which clear'd the *Rhine* of the *French* to *Philipſbourgh*. From *Bonn* he march'd with thoſe Troops to *Limburg*, which alſo ſurrender'd in a ſhort Time: After which he came and join'd the Veldt-Marſhal. Whilſt the Duke was employ'd in taking theſe Places, the Duke *de Villeroy* came at the Head of the *French* Army, to try what he could do with the Veldt-Marſhal, who, upon *Villeroy*'s advancing, drew under the Cannon of *Maſtricht*; notwithſtanding which he drew up his Army within Cannon Shot of us, and made a Show as if he would attack us, and fell to cannonading with great Fury; but what with the Cannon of our Camp, thoſe from the Works of the Town, and from *Petersburg*, ſoon made him weary, and oblig'd him to draw off. On the Duke's joining us he march'd within Lines, where he kept the remaining Part of the Campaign.

The Duke follow'd, and encamp'd about a League from him. Theſe Lines were prodigious ſtrong, and extended from *Namur* to *Antwerp*, that took in all the *Spaniſh Netherlands*. While we lay here the Duke ſent a Detachment to take in *Huy* on the *Maeſe*, half Way between *Liege* and *Namur*, which Place ſurrender'd in about a Fortnight; ſo that now the Elector of *Cologn* had not one Place left him in his whole Electorate except *Guelders*, which being ſituated in a Moraſs, and not eaſy to come at, a Blockade was form'd about it, which it ſtood almoſt a Year, and then ſurrender'd. After the taking of *Huy*, the Duke

of the Duke of Marlborough.

Duke made several Marches and Countermarches 1703. along the Lines, to try if he could get within them, but to no Purpose; for *Villeroy* kept such a watchful Eye on all his Motions that the could make nothing of it. The remaining Part of this Campaign past without any other Action, than that between *Boufflers* and *Opdam* at *Eckerengen*: Both Armies went to Quarters about the Middle of *October*.

The Elector of *Bavaria*, whose Ambition led him to no less than the Imperial Crown, had last Year, with the Assistance of *France*, carried all before him in the Empire, and in all Probability would this Year have drove the Emperor out of *Vienna*, had not the Duke of *Marlborough* undertaken his glorious Expedition into *Germany*, which he carried on with so much Secrefy, that puzzled all the Politicians of the *French* Court to find out his Designs. He came over early this Spring, and after consulting with the 1704. *States General* on this great Undertaking, he gave Orders for the Troops in these Parts, that were to act under him, to march and assemble at *Roremund*, where we arrived the Beginning of *May*; from whence we march'd to *Juliers*, where the Duke came and took a Review of these Troops; but more particularly of the *British* Troops of our Nation, whom we found to be 19 Squadrons of Horse and Dragoons, and 14 Battalions, computed to be about 14,000 effective Men. From *Juliers* we continued by several Marches thro' the Electorate of *Cologn* to *Coblentz*, where we were join'd by the *Prussian* and *Hanoverian* Auxiliaries.

It had been given out that we were to act on the *Moselle*, and not only our own Army, but even the Court of *France* did the same; wherefore they order'd the Marshal *Villeroy* to march with 40,000 Men from the *Netherlands* to the *Moselle*, and he was by

this

1704. Time arriv'd at *Treves*. This March of *Villeroy*'s freed the *States* from the Apprehensions they were under of the *French* over-running their Frontiers when the *Duke* was march'd off.

We halted here two Days; after which to the Surprize of us all, we crofs'd the *Mofelle* and the *Rhine* both at this Place, and march'd through the Country of *Heffe-Caffel*, where we were join'd by the Hereditary Prince of that Country with a Body Body of *Heffians*, which compleated the Duke's Army to 40,000. Having pafs'd through *Heffe*, we march'd through the Electorate of *Mentz*, and fo through the *Palatinate* of the *Rhine*, till we came to *Heidelberg*; here we halted four Days, nor was it publickly known, till we came here, whither the Duke defign'd.

From hence we march'd through the Country of *Wirtemberg*, towards the *Danube*. *June* 16, O. S. we join'd the Imperial Army, under Prince *Lewis* of *Baden*, at *Gingen* or *Hefpach*. A grand Council of War was held, wherein it was agreed that the Prince of *Baden*, in Conjunction with the Duke of *Marlborough*, fhould act againft the Elector of *Bavaria*, and that they fhould command alternately; while Prince *Eugene* obferv'd the Motions of *Villeroy*, who had hitherto obferv'd the March of my Lord *Marlborough*, and was now arriv'd at *Strafburg* on the *Rhine*.

The 19th our two Generals took a View of their Army, and found them to be about 80,000. The 20th, we march'd and encamp'd within Sight of the Elector and Marfhal *Marfhin*, who commanded the *French* that had join'd his Camp at *Dillingen*, a ftrong Poft on this Side the *Danube*; their Army were 70,000. The Elector apprehending our Generals had a Defign upon *Donawert*, fent off this Evening Count *d'Acro* with 18,000 Men to fecure that Poft. Our Generals finding there was no attacking the Enemy in the Poft they were in, marched

of the Duke of Marlborough. 45

next Morning to *Hermerdingen*, leaving the Elector 1704.
behind us. The 22d of *June*, O. S. the Duke's
Day of Command, he march'd by Three in the
Morning at the Head of 30 Squadrons, three Regiments of Imperial Grenadiers, and a Detachment of
7000 Foot, the whole Army marching close after
him, and as we march'd off from the Left the *British*
Troops led the Van. About Noon the Duke came
up to the River *Wrentz*, a League from *Donawert*;
which being a deep still River, and the Enemy having broke down the Bridge, took the Duke some
Hours to repair and lay others, that it was past Four
before he got to *Donawert*, where he found Count
Acro hard at Work in fortifying the Hill of *Schullingberg*, which lay close to this Town, on which he
form'd a Disposition for attacking. About Six o'Clock
all the *British* Troops being come, he order'd the
Attack to be made. The Enemy maintain'd their
Posts with great Obstinacy for an Hour and ten
Minutes, but at Length were forced to give Way,
when our Men made a most terrible Slaughter.
Count *Acro*, with the greatest Part of them made
down the Back of the Hill to the *Danube*, where was
a Bridge of Boats, but the Crowds pressing on it,
it broke, by which great Numbers were drown'd.

The Count, with several Officers of Note, saved
themselves by their Horses swimming the River.
This Loss was computed to be about 7000 kill'd, 2000
drown'd, and 4000 made Prisoners; with the Loss
of all their Artillery, Tents and Baggage. Our Loss
was also very considerable, having near 5000 kill'd
and wounded.

When the Elector saw us pass his Camp at *Dillingen*, he cross'd the *Danube*, and made what Haste
he could to succour *Acro*, but arriv'd only Time
enough to behold his Fate. He turn'd to the Right

and

1704. and march'd to *Aufburg*, where he strongly intrench'd himself under the Cannon of that City, and sent an Express to *Villeroy* to send him forthwith a strong Reinforcement, or all must be lost: On which *Villeroy* sent off the Marshal *Tallard*, with 60 Squadrons and 40 Battalions of the best Troops he had.

On the Elector's turning to *Aufburg*, he sent to the Governor of *Donawert* to set Fire to the Magazines, which were very confiderable, and retire; this must have set the whole Town on Fire; wherefore the Magistrates found Means to give our Generals timely Notice, on which early next Morning they order'd Bridges to be laid both above and below the Town, to cut off his Retreat; which the Governor perceiving, had only Time to set Fire to one of the Magazines and fled. The Inhabitants soon stifled the Fire, and threw open their Gates.

We halted here two Days after the Action, and passing the *Danube* march'd towards the *Leck*, which bounds *Bavaria* from *Swabia*; and having pass'd this River, we came to a small fortify'd Town call'd *Rain*, which took us four Days: And being in the Country of *Bavaria*, Parties were sent abroad to plunder the Country, but not set Fire to any Place. This our Generals did to try if it would draw off the Elector from the Interest of *France*, which had that Effect, that it set a Treaty on Foot for that Purpose; and a Stop was put to our plundering Parties. As soon as *Rain* surrender'd we march'd to *Heidelberg*, which was the utmost Extent of our March into *Germany*.

This was within a League of *Aufburg*, from whence we had a fair View of that City and the Elector's Camp; we lay here about a Month, during which Time the Treaty was carried on, and our Generals had great Hopes of its succeeding, but all this was
only

of the Duke of Marlborough.   47

only Grimace; for as soon as the Elector had an Account that *Tallard* was got through the *Black-Forest*, and arriv'd at *Ulm*, he abruptly broke off the Treaty. Our Generals finding themselves thus imposed on, sent Parties to plunder and burn all the Villages and Towns as far as the Gates of *Munich*.

1704.

The Elector was an Eye-witness of the Calamity of his Country, which irritated him to Revenge more than mollify'd him to Compassion; wherefore on his joining *Tallard*, he resolv'd to vent his Fury on the Country of *Wirtemberg*.

On our second Day's March, just as we were pitching our Camp, Prince *Eugene*, who march'd from the *Rhine* with 20,000 Men to observe *Tallard*'s March thro' the *Black-Forest*, and had left them under the Command of the Duke of *Wirtemberg* at the strong Camp of *Munster*, came riding along our Line, and went to the Duke's Quarters, where they settled the Operations of the Campaign, and form'd a Scheme for sending the Prince of *Baden* out of their Way; who being an old captious General, was not for running Hazards. The Duke of *Marlborough*'s Case was such, that unless he did something more to free the Empire from the War, he knew what his Fate would be upon his Return to *England*; and Prince *Eugene* being a successful pushing General, and who plainly saw that unless something extraordinary was done while the Duke was in the *Empire*, the Elector of *Bavaria* would at length carry the Imperial Crown, and then all *Europe* must submit to him and the *French* King; so that this was the critical Juncture, on which not only the Fate of the *Empire*, but that of *Europe* depended.

Prince *Eugene* and the Duke having thoroughly weigh'd these Matters went to the Prince of *Baden*'s Quarters, and proposed to him his undertaking the

Siege

1704. Siege of *Ingoldstadt* with 20,000 *Germans*, and the Duke at the same Time march'd with the rest of the Army, and join'd Prince *Eugene*'s Troops at *Munster*, where our Generals had an Account of the Junction of the Elector and *Tallard*, and of their passing the *Danube* at *Lawengen*, which was about six Leagues off our Camp. Next Morning our Generals rode at the Head of a strong Body of Horse in order to mark out a Camp on the Plains of *Hockstet*, but when they came within Sight of it, they perceiv'd the Enemies Quarter-Masters laying out a Camp on it, and the Front of their Army entering the Plains. Our Generals stay'd some Time to observe their Manner of Incampment, and then return'd with a Resolution of giving them Battle next Day, and as soon as they return'd to Camp, they gave Orders for striking our Tents, and to send them with all the Baggage to the Hill of *Schulenberg*, and prepare for Battle. Next Morning being the 2d of *August*, O. S. or 13th, N. S. our Army, consisting of 181 Squadrons and 67 Battalions, march'd by Break of Day in Eight Columns to the Enemy, who were about three Leagues from us.

The Duke of *Marlborough* receiv'd the Sacrament this Morning, and on mounting his Horse said, *This Day I conquer, or die*. A noble Instance of the Christian and the Hero.

When we came within Sight of the Enemy, Prince *Eugene* with the Imperialists stretch'd away to the Right, and drew opposite the Elector, and Part of the Troops under *Marsin*; and the Duke with the Troops he brought up with him, stretch'd to the Left, and drew up opposite *Tallard*, and the Right of *Marsin*. About eight o'Clock we began to form our Lines, at which Time the Enemy set Fire to all the Villages that might be of any Cover to us, and

of the Duke of Marlborough. 49

the Cannon on both Sides began to fire with great Fury. 1706.

The Elector, *Tallard*, and *Marsin*, went to the Top of the Steeple of *Blenheim*, from whence they had a fair View of our whole Army: The Elector and *Marsin* were for drawing the Army as close to the marshy Ground they had in their Front, as was possible, and not suffer a Man over but on the Points of their Bayonets; but *Tallard*, a haughty proud *Frenchman*, was of a different Opinion, for he said, that would be no more than making a drawn Battle of it. Therefore he said, the only Way to get a compleat Victory would be to draw up their Army at some small Distance from the Morass, and suffer us to come over to them, and the more that came over the more they were sure to kill.

Neither the Elector nor *Marsin* could persuade him out of this Notion; they both very much dissatisfied, and, dreading the Consequence, left him, and went to their Posts.

When our Army came in Sight of them, their whole Camp was standing, which they soon struck, and sent to the Town of *Hockstet*, about half a Mile in their Rear.

The Situation of the Ground and Disposition of the French *Army.*

They had on their Right the River *Danube*, and the Village *Blenheim* standing close on the Bank of it; on their Left was a large thick Wood, from whence runs a small Rivulet which empties itself into the *Danube* at *Blenheim*; this Rivulet made the Ground along their Front in most Places very Marshy. In giving an Account of this Battle, I shall be the more particular, in relating what past between the Duke of *Marlborough* and Marshal *Tallard*, between whom

D the

the greatest Stress of it was fought. When *Tallard* found our General's Resolution for attacking them, which at first he could hardly believe, he to make sure Work on his Side, threw into the Village of *Blenheim* 28 Battalions and 12 Squadrons of Dragoons commanded by the Marquis *de Hautville*, who had Orders, that when he found our Army pass the marshy Ground, he was then to march out and fall on our Rear, by which *Tallard* proposed to have us between two Fires, and then he could not fail of what he proposed; he also order'd two more of his Battalions with six of those under *Marsin* into the Village of *Aberclaw*, which lay towards their Centre; these were also to march out and join the Troops from *Blenheim*; he also placed some Foot in the two Mills that stood on the Rivulet between *Blenheim* and *Aberclaw*.

The rest of his Troops, being 48 Squadrons and ten Battalions, he drew upon the Heighth of the Plain near half a Mile from the marshy Ground, to give our Troops an Opportunity of passing over to him. This was the Disposition *Tallard* made of his 60 Squadrons and 40 Battalions which he brought from the *Rhine*. But the Elector and *Marsin* made a quite different Disposition of their Troops; for they drew up close to the marshy Ground, and would not suffer a Man to come over to them. Thus was their whole Army form'd for receiving us, which consisted of 163 Squadrons and 83 Battalions, with 120 Cannon and Mortars; and we had but 64: So that our Army was 18 Squadrons more than they, and their Army 16 Battalions more than ours.

The Duke of *Marlborough* observing the Disposition *Tallard* had made, saw immediately what he design'd; whereupon he order'd General *Churchill*, with 19 Battalions to attack the Village of *Blenheim*,

of the Duke of Marlborough.

and Lieutenant-General *Wood*, with eight Squadrons to support him in Case of Need. Here all our *British* Infantry were engag'd: He also order'd Prince *Holstein-beck*, with six Battalions to attack the Village of *Aberclaw*, and two Battalions to attack the Mills.

A little before One the Signal was given, at which Time Brigadier *Roe*, at the Head of two *British* Brigades, led on the Attack of *Blenheim*, but were repuls'd with confiderable Lofs. The Brigadier himfelf was kill'd, and the Brigades purfued by fome Horfe that were on the Flank of the Village; but upon the coming up of the reft of our Infantry, their Horfe retreated, and the two Brigades being foon rallied, came again to the Charge, fo that we drove the Enemy from the Skirts of the Village into the Body of it, which they had fortify'd after the beft Manner they could in fo fhort a Time; in which this great Body of Troops were fo pent up and crowded, that they had not Room to make Ufe of their Arms. We made feveral Attempts to force in upon them, but could not, in which we loft a great many brave Officers and Soldiers, whofe Lives might have been faved, had General *Churchill*, and a great many others of our warm Generals been advifed to have halted where we were forced to do it at laft, which was about 150 Paces from them, where we drew up in great Order ready to receive them when they offered to come out upon us, by which they were fo hemm'd in, that they were of no further Ufe to their Army this Day, tho' they have been blamed by a great many, for not forcing themfelves thro' us, and join *Tallard* in the Field: but thofe that were of that Opinion knew nothing of the Matter; for, confidering the Situation they were in, it was impoffible for them to draw up in any Manner of Order.

But suppose they could, they must be put into great Disorder in coming out over the Works they had made; so that before they could put themselves into any Order to attack us they would be mow'd down by our Platoons, which they found by Experience; for they made several Attempts to come out upon us, but we cut them down as fast as they appeared: so that, had there been double their Number, it was impossible for them to force their Way, considering the Order we were in to receive them.

Thus was this great Body of *Tallard*'s Army rendred incapable of doing him any Service in the Field, where he very much wanted them.

Let us suppose what the Duke was doing in other Places; all that Prince *Holstein-beck* had to do was to prevent the Troops in *Aberclaw* from coming out.

The Duke having thus secured himself from the Attack in the Rear, he then ordered Col. *Palmes*, with three *English* Squadrons of Horse to pass over before him; who not meeting with the least Opposition, drew up on the other Side at some Distance from the marshy Ground, to give Room for our Lines to form behind him.

The Duke followed *Palmes*; the Mills were attack'd, but those that were in them set them on Fire, and made off: Both Cavalry and Infantry which the Duke kept with him in the Field, which were not above 10 or 12 Battalions, passed over as well as they could, and formed as fast as they got over: *Tallard* all this while, as a Man infatuated, stood looking on, without suffering either great or small Shot to be fired at them; only when he saw *Palmes* advanced towards him, he order'd five (some say seven) Squadrons to march down, and cut those three Squadrons to Pieces, and so return. The Officer that commanded

of the Duke of Marlborough.

1704.

commanded the *French* Squadrons, as soon as he had got clear of the Line, ordered the Squadrons on his right and left to edge outward, and then to wheel in upon the Flanks of *Palmes*; which *Palmes* perceiving, ordered Major *Oldfield*, who commanded the Squadron on his right, and Major *Creed*, who commanded that on his left, to wheel outwards, and charge the Squadrons coming down upon them. And not in the least doubting their beating of them, ordered them, when they had done that, to wheel in upon the Flanks of the others; and he at the same time would charge them in the Front. Accordingly every thing succeeded; so that these three Squadrons drove their five or seven back to their Army. This was the first Action in the Field, which took up some Time, and gave the Duke an Opportunity of forming his Lines; and now there was a fair Plain, without Hedge or Ditch, for the Cavalry on both Sides to shew their Bravery; there being but few of the Infantry to interpose, and they drawn up separately from the Horse.

When *Tallard* saw so many of his Squadrons beaten by three, he was strangely confounded; whereupon he advanced with all his Cavalry to charge the Duke, at which time he expected the Troops in the Villages would have marched out, and fallen on his Rear; but the Duke having taken effectual Means to prevent that, was now advancing with his Squadrons to meet him.

The *Gendarmes* (of which *Tallard*'s Horse mostly consisted, and in whom he placed his greatest Confidence, believing there was not any Troops in the World able to stand before them) began the Battle, giving a most furious Charge, and broke thro' Part of our Front-Line; but the second Line coming up made them retreat faster than they came on, which cooled

cooled those Gentlemen's Courage, for they never made such another Charge; upon which our Squadrons advanced, and charged in their Turn: And thus they charged each other for some Time with various Success, till at length the *French* Courage began to abate, and charged but faintly; so that they gave Ground as our Squadrons advanced, till they got on the Height where they were first drawn up: where their ten Battalions had stood while the Horse were engaged, but now advanced, and interposed with their Fire; which put a Stop to our Squadrons, till our Foot and Col. *Blood*'s, with nine Field-Pieces laden with small Shot, came up, which kept them employ'd. This gave a Respite of Time to the Squadrons on both Sides to put themselves into Order, after the Hurry and Confusion that constantly attend such Actions. During which Time, *Tallard* sent to *Blenheim*, for those Troops to come out to join him; but they were neither able to help him, nor themselves: He also sent to *Marsin*, but he sent him Word, that he had too much Work on his own Hands.

The Duke of *Marlborough*, after this Breathing-Time, being freed from the Fire of their Foot; and finding their Horse had no great Stomach for renewing the Battle, but rather seemed in a tottering Condition, gave Orders to all his Cavalry to make a Home-Charge upon them, which they did with such Resolution, that it decided the Fate of the Day; for they were not able to stand this Charge; and our Squadrons breaking thro' their very Centre, put them to an entire Retreat: thirty of their Squadrons fled towards a Bridge they had on the *Danube* between *Blenheim* and *Hochstet*; but by a Crowd rushing upon it, it broke, and our Squadrons pursuing with great Fury, very few, which made that Way, escap'd being

of the Duke of Marlborough.

being kill'd, or drowned. *Tallard* himself made that Way, but finding the Bridge broke, he returned up the River towards *Hochstet*, but was taken before he got thither: the rest of their Horse made towards *Lavingen*, but were not pursued far; 13 Battalions were all cut to Pieces, to a Man, not one of them escaping, but such as threw themselves down among the Slain; I rode thro' them next Morning as they lay dead in Rank and File.

No General did ever behave with more Calmness of Temper, and Presence of Mind, than did the Duke of *Marlborough* on this Occasion; he was in all Places wherever his Presence was requisite, without Fear of Danger, or in the least Hurry, giving his Orders with all the Calmness imaginable.

Now let us see what was doing between Prince *Eugene*, the Elector, and *Marsin*.

As I said before, those two Generals stood at the very Brink of the marshy Ground; and all that Prince *Eugene* could do, could not force them to give an Inch of Ground, till the Duke having dispatch'd *Tallard*, and was drawing some Squadrons that Way, which the Elector and *Marsin* perceiving, and finding *Tallard* draw out of the Field, they immediately put themselves on the Retreat, by readily forming their Troops into three Columns, and march'd off with great Dexterity and Expedition.

By this time the Duke was drawing down to fall on them as they march'd off; but a Body of Troops being observed in the Rear of them, and their Cavalry, which form'd a Column to cover the Infantry, marching in great Order, he halted, believing these in the Rear to be a Rear-Guard they had form'd to cover their Retreat; and Prince *Eugene* by this time having got a good Body of his Troops over, and just ready to fall on their Rear, seeing the Duke's

1704. Squadrons marching down, took them to be some of *Tallard*'s coming to join the Elector, which occasioned him to halt, for the rest of his Troops to come over to him; upon which our Generals sent their Aid de Camps to know how Matters stood with each of them; in the mean time the Elector and *Marsin* got over the Pass of *Morstingen*, Night coming on, and our Troops very much fatigued, our Generals pursued no farther. The Troops in *Blenheim* seeing their Army drove out of the Field, surrendred at Discretion, but those in *Auberclaw* made a Shift to get off with *Marsin*.

Thus have I given the most exact Account of this famous Battle, that I could possibly gather from the strictest Enquiry I could make among the Troops that had engaged in most Parts: for next Morning I rode thro' the greatest Part of the Field of Battle, where I made the best Remarks and Observations to inform myself of it.

The Loss of the Enemy was computed to be about 40,000, kill'd, drowned, and taken, with all their Artillery, Tents, and Baggage, besides a very great Booty. Our Army had near 14,000 kill'd and wounded: those under Prince *Eugene* suffered most. I shall say nothing as to the Consequences that attended this famous Battle, more than that it decided the Fate of the Empire, fixed the Imperial Crown in the House of *Austria*, and was the first fatal Blow that *Lewis* XIV. had received during his whole Reign.

The Elector and *Marsin* continued their March all the Night, and never made a Halt till they got to *Ulm*, where they staid but one Day, and then made the best of their Way thro' the *Black Forest*, and so joined *Villeroy* on the *Rhine*.

The

of the Duke of Marlborough.

The Afternoon after the Battle our Army marched to *Lawingen*, where we halted till our Tents and Baggage came to us, and then marched to *Ulm*, from whence we marched in four Columns thro' the Country of *Wirtemberg*, and joined again at *Philipsburg*; there we passed the *Rhine*, and encamped on *Spireback*, a Place remarkable for a Victory obtained the preceding Year by *Tallard* over the Prince of *Hesse*.

Our two Generals waited here for the coming of the Prince of *Baden*, who could never forgive them for robbing him of a Share of the Glory of the late Victory, to whom *Imgoldstadt* surrendred, as soon as they heard of the Defeat of their Army; he arrived about the 20th of *August*, O.S. as did also all the Troops that were guarding the Lines towards *Strasbourg*, which compleated our Army to 135,000 Men; whereupon it was agreed, that Prince *Lewis* with all the Troops that were not in the Battle should lay Siege to the unfortunate Town of *Landau*; and to carry on the same under the King of the *Romans*, who was at this time upon his Departure from *Vienna*; whilst the Duke and Prince *Eugene* with their Troops were to march to *Cronwessenberg*, and there to cover the Siege.

Villeroy had drawn all the Troops he could muster up to *Landau*, to try if he could prevent its falling into the Hands of the Allies; but, on the Approach of our Army, he marched off, and never offered the least Disturbance after,

While the Siege of *Landau* was carrying on, the Duke of *Marlborough* considering the great Difficulties he would have in carrying on the Siege and War in the *Netherlands*, which was crouded with a Number of the best fortify'd Towns in *Europe*, besides the strong Lines which surrounded them, had now formed a Scheme for carrying on the War along the

Mossel,

Moffel, thro' the Countries of *Luxemberg* and *Lorrain*.

Whereupon it was agreed in a Council of War, that Prince *Lewis* of *Baden*, with 40,000 *Imperialists*, should early next Spring join the Duke on the *Moffel*; upon this, the Duke ordered the Prince of *Heffe* to march with the *Pruffian*, *Hannoverian*, and *Heffian* Troops, that were in *British* Pay, towards *Treves*, himself going along with them, where, after he had taken in that City, and cleared the *Moffel* of all the *French* Garrisons from thence to *Coblentz*, he returned to *Cronweffenberg*, leaving the Prince with his Troops to take Care of those Quarters for the Winter.

Laudau held out till the latter End of *November*; but the Duke finding it was not in the Power of the Enemy to raise the Siege, sent off the *British* and *Dutch* Troops about the Middle of *October*. The Infantry went down the *Rhine* in Boats as far as *Nimeguen*, from whence they dispersed into Quarters, and the Cavalry marched by Land the same Way they came up.

In the Beginning of *May*, according to the Scheme the Duke of *Marlboro'* had formed at *Cronweffenberg*, he marched from *Maftricht* with the same Number of Troops as last Year, thro' the Country of *Limburg*, up to the *Moffel*, and encamped off that River two Leagues above *Treves*, where the Prince of *Heffe* join'd him with those Troops the Duke left with him. Here the Prince of *Baden* was to have joined him; but the *Germans* being now freed from the *Bavarian* War, were backward in sending their Quotas so early into the Field as they ought to have done, and Prince *Eugene* having been obliged to go into *Italy* with a Body of Troops to assist the Duke of *Savoy*, as he was like to be hard pressed this Summer by *France*; all which prevented the Prince of
Baden

of the Duke of Marlborough. 59

Baden from joining the Duke, as it had been agreed 1705.
upon: However, he gave the Duke Hopes, that in
a little time he would be able to join him at *Elft*;
upon which the Duke crossed the *Moffel* and the
Saar, and marched to the Defile of *Taveren*, and
advanced to *Elft*, where he waited upwards of a
Month for the coming of the Prince: but whether it
was for the Want of the *German* Troops, or the
Grudge he bore him on account of the Battle of
Hochstet, or both together, he at length sent Word
he could not come.

Marshal *Villars* commanded the *French* Army in
these Parts, who lay strongly encamped at *Sirk*, two
Leagues from us, with 70,000 Men; and tho' our
Army did not exceed 40,000, yet he never offer'd
the least Disturbance. During this time the Duke
was hard press'd by the Elector of *Bavaria* and *Villeroy*
in the *Netherlands*, where the Velt-Marshal had
not an Army sufficient to oppose them: for they had
by this time taken *Huy*, and were marching to *Liege*,
whereupon the States sent an Express to the Duke,
praying him to make what Haste back he could to
their Assistance.

Thus was the Duke of *Marlboro'* disappointed in
the noble Scheme he had formed for carrying the War
thro' *Lorrain* into the Heart of *France*: for, had
Prince *Lewis* performed his Part, the *Netherlands*
would soon be drained of the *French* to defend themselves
at home. The Duke having received this
Express, prepared for marching back with what Expedition
he could; and being apprehensive that *Villars*
might attempt falling on his Rear, as he was
passing the Defile of *Taveren*, he therefore, on beating
Tattoo, decamp'd, and march'd all the Night;
and by the time it was Day, seeing none of *Villars*'s
Troops appear, we entred the Defile, and passed it

without

without the least Molestation from *Villars*, tho' he was near double our Number. Having got thro' this dangerous Defile, which was a narrow Passage between two Mountains, more than a League in Length, the Duke proceeded to the *Netherlands* with all the Expedition he could; so that we were not above half the Time returning that we were in going. When we came near *Aix la Chapelle*, the Duke received an Express from the Velt-Marshal, that the Enemy were in Possession of the City of *Liege*, and carrying on a vigorous Siege against the Citadel; on which he march'd off with the Horse and Dragoons, with all the Grenadiers behind them, leaving Orders with General *Churchill* to make what Haste he could with the Infantry after him. The Duke joined the Veldt-Marshal that Evening at *Petersburgh*, but the Elector and *Villeroy* hearing of it, early next Morning marched off from *Liege*, and never halted till they got within their Lines.

As soon as our Infantry joined the Duke, he march'd after the Enemy, and encamp'd within a League of their Lines, each Army being about 80,000; from hence the Duke sent a Detachment to retake *Huy*; during which Time he had formed a Scheme for passing the Lines, which we managed as follows: The Elector and *Villeroy* finding the Duke encamped so near their Lines, did imagine he had a Design to surprize them by some sudden Attempt; wherefore, they drew as close together as they conveniently could, leaving only small Guards to take Care of the Lines on each Side of them.

The Detachment being returned after taking *Huy*, the Duke put his Project in Execution.

The Enemy had the *Mehaign* about half a League on their right, and about three Leagues on their

left

of the Duke of Marlborough.

left they had two Barriers for the Conveniency of the Country People paffing to and fro.

The Duke got in with a Gentleman whofe Eftate lay in thofe Parts, therefore wanted the *French* out of his Neighbourhood, and their Lines demolifh'd; this Gentleman acquainted the Duke with the Barriers, and procured him trufty Guides to direct him in the Night to them.

Whereupon on the 6th of *July*, O. S. about Noon, the Veldt-Marfhal decamp'd, and march'd with the *Dutch* Troops towards the *Mehaign*, and foon after the reft of the Army ftruck their Tents, and lay on their Arms, at which Time a Detachment of 10,000 Men under the Command of Count *Noailles* and Lieutenant General *Ingoldsby* were ordered to draw up on the Right of the Army, where they alfo lay down on their Arms. The Enemy foon had an Account of all this, from whence they concluded that the Duke had a Defign of attacking them by Break of Day next Morning, and made a Difpofition accordingly to receive us. *Villeroy* moved towards his Right to obferve the Veldt-Marfhal, and the Elector with their Left Wing, edg'd to the Right to make good his Ground, there they lay on their Arms all Night, expecting us in the Morning.

As foon as it grew dark, *Noailles* and *Ingoldsby* marched with their Detachment away towards the Right to the Barriers, having a good many Pioneers with them; the Army followed clofe after them, and the Veldt Marfhal at the fame time faced about, and made what Hafte he could after us.

Thus we continued marching all the Night. By the Time Day appeared, *Noailles* and *Ingoldsby* came up to the Barriers, where they found only a Lieutenant and forty Men guarding each of them, who giving one fire, fcour'd off; upon which they
entered

1705. entered the Lines and drew up on the other side, and the Pioneers fell to work in throwing them down, and enlarging the Entrance.

The Duke, who kept at the Head of the Right Wing of Horse, and close to the Detachment, past immediately, and drew up the Squadrons as fast as they got over.

The Enemy a little before had got some Notice of our March and Design, whereupon the Elector ordered the Marquis *D'Allegar* and Count *Horne*, with the left Wing of their Cavalry to march with all the Expedition they could, to prevent our passing the Lines at the Barriers, while the Elector followed with the Infantry; but when *D'Allegar* and *Horne* came near the Barriers, they found the Duke at the Head of his Cavalry ready to receive them; however, they march'd resolutely down, and the Duke advanced easily to meet them, ordering the Infantry as they past to follow him. The Enemy charged with great Resolution; but were repulsed, and obliged to retire. By this Time the Elector arrived with part of his Infantry, on which he advanced and repulsed the Charge.

The greatest Part of our Infantry on the right Wing, being now got over, drew up behind the Horse. The Duke receiv'd the Elector in his Charge, and broke thro' his Squadrons, and was advancing briskly after them, but was stopt by the Fire of some Foot that were privately posted in a hollow Way; on which our Foot came up, and drove them from thence. The Elector by this Time had rallied his Squadrons, and the Duke now advanced upon him, and charged him with such Resolution that entirely broke all his Squadrons, and put them to the Rout; so abandoning the Foot they had with them, they fled outright, and never rallied more.

Here

of the Duke of Marlborough.   63

Here it was, that the ten *Bavarian* Battalions threw 1705.
themselves into the Hollow Square, and march'd off
in Spite of all our Cavalry, our Foot being so very
much fatigued, that they could not possibly get up
to them. This shews what Resolution and keeping
good Order can do.

Villeroy was making what Haste he could to assist
the Elector; but finding him defeated, he turned
short, and made the best of his Way to *Lovain*,
where he found him with the Remains of his shattered
Troops of the left Wing. The Duke having thus
baffled the Enemy out of those prodigious Lines,
halted for the coming up of the Veldt-Marshal, whose
Troops were so very much fatigued, that we could
not possibly follow the Enemy, but lay on our Arms
here all Night, nor could we march after them till
twelve next Day. Upon our coming up to *Lovain*
we found the Enemy encamp'd on the other side the
Dyle, a deep, still River, running thro' the Town,
with marshy Grounds on each side of it. After we
had lain incamp'd within Cannon Shot of them about
ten Days, the Duke made an Attempt for passing the
River about two Leagues above the Town; but the
Enemy being now much more on their Guard, than
when in their Lines, got thither time enough to prevent it. After this he made another Attempt to pass
at the Head of the *Dyle*; but on his coming he found
them so posted, that he withdrew again; whereupon
he spent the remaining part of the Campaign in levelling the Lines to the Ground.

In the Beginning of *May*, the Duke assembled the 1706.
Army at *Burklone* near *Maestricht*, where he had an
Account that the Elector and *Villeroy* were assembling
the *French* Army on the Plains of Mount *St. Andrea*,
on which the Duke advanced to *Hannoy*, which
brought the Enemy to *Ramellies*, which was but
three

1706. three Leagues from us; whereupon the Duke, the very next Morning, being the 12th of *May*, O. S. and *Whitfunday*, without waiting for the *Danish* Horse, that were almost a Day's March behind, advanc'd in eight Columns to the Enemy, our Army consisting only of 117 Squadrons, the *Danish* Horse included, and 80 Battalions. The Enemy had 132 Squadrons and 90 Battalions. The Elector and *Villeroy* with two Enginiers, under Pretence of Hunting, having viewed all the Ground from *Lovain* to the *Main*, pitched on *Ramillies* for giving Battle to the Duke of *Marlbro'*; whereupon they made the Enginiers draw a Plan of the Ground, with a Disposition of the Order of Battle, and sent it to Court by one of the Enginiers, for the King's Approbation; the King seemed highly pleased, and all his Politicians, with the Scheme; and were in Hopes it would give a Check to the Duke of *Marlborough*'s Successes; he therefore ordered them such a Number of Troops, as they required, wherein were a great part of the Houshold. The Nature of the Ground and Disposition they made of their Army was thus, *viz*. They had the *Main* on their Right, with the Village *Tavier* on the Banks of it; a little from thence was the Village *Franquinier*; into those Villages they threw a good Body of Foot and Dragoons, their Horses being link'd at a small Distance behind them. Between the Villages were two Lines of Foot interlined with some Dragoons. From *Franquinier* to the Village of *Ramillies*, a fine Plain, on which they drew up most of their best Cavalry, interlined with their best Infantry, and drawn up in three Lines; here they knew the main Stress of the Battle must be fought; therefore they crowded all their best Troops. In the Village of *Ramillies*, which lay something to the left of their Center, they placed twenty Battalions

of the Duke of Marlborough.

with some Cannon, as they had done in the other Villages. From *Ramillies* runs the River *Geet*, which makes the Ground in most Places very swampy; along this River they drew up only a single Line of their Infantry, which extended to *Offuse*, and so on to *Auteregliers*, which covered their left Flank. This was the Situation and Disposition the Duke of *Marlbro'* found the Enemy in when he came up to them.

There was a rising Ground on our side of them, from whence the Duke had a fair View of their Disposition; and at once, that the Stress of the Battle must fall in the Plain, where they appeared very formidable; wherefore he immediately form'd a Scheme for obliging them to break thro' all their fine Plan; so that, in less than an Hour, without firing a Shot, he obliged them to break their Disposition in the Centre, where they had placed the great Dependence of the Success of the Battle.

The Right of our Army drew up on this rising Ground, opposite their Left, along the *Geet*, from whence our Line extended into the Plain, and so on to the *Mehaign*.

The Duke observing the Enemies Left so thinly man'd, and tho' he plainly saw there was no attacking them in that Part, yet the first thing he did was to order our right Wing to march down, as if he designed to attack them first there. This answered what he expected; for as soon as the Elector and *Villeroy* saw our right Wing marching down on their Left, they were startled; whereupon they in a great Hurry sent off from the Plain a great many of those Troops to sustain their Left, which put the rest on the Plain into some Disorder, in making good the Ground of those that march'd off. The Duke ordered our Right to retire easily back without altering our Aspect, which we did, till the Rear Line had got on the Back of the rising Ground, out of Sight of the Enemy; at which Time the front Line halted; and the Duke sent Orders to the Rear Line to face to the Left, and march with what Expedition they could away to the Centre; this the Enemy did not in the least perceive. The Duke having thus brought Matters to bear, rides down to the Centre, whither he had ordered the greatest part of his Cavalry, as well as Infantry to be drawn up; and after he had put all things in order for attacking the Enemy, he sent to the Veldt-Marshal to begin the Battle on the Left with the *Dutch* Infantry, their Cavalry being drawn away to the Center. As soon as the Veldt-Marshal had begun the Battle, the Duke ordered four Brigades of Foot to attack the Village of *Ramillies*, which being done, he ordered the Squadrons and Foot in the Center to advance and charge the Enemy in the Plain.

Here the Cavalry charged each other for a considerable time with various Success, the Foot on both sides often stopping the Squadrons in their Career. The Duke finding the Enemy maintain their Ground with great Resolution, ordered all his Squadrons to advance briskly, and give them a Home Charge. In this Hurry the Duke was unhorsed, and in great Danger of his Life, but Col. *Bringfield* his Gentleman of Horse being at hand with led Horses, soon remounted him; but as he was holding the Duke's Stirrup, a Cannon Ball took off his Head. At the Time our Cavalry made this Home Charge on the Enemy, up comes the Duke of *Wirtemberg* with the *Danish* Horse, who falling on their Flank next to the Village of *Franquenier*, charg'd them with such Fury that it put them into great Disorder, and pursuing his Blow drove them on their Center, which put the Whole into Confusion. The Duke did not slip this Op-

of the Duke of Marlborough.

Opportunity, but preffed home till he put them to the Rout. The Elector and *Villeroy* did all they could to keep up the Troops, but in vain. The Houfhold Troops, who had hitherto behaved with great Bravery, rallied and came again to the Charge; but the *French* Fire, which on all firft Onfets feems very furious, was now fpent; and befides, their light Horfe took to Flight, and could never be brought to rally, fo the Houfhold were forced to follow, abandoning their Foot to the Fury of our Troops, to be cut to Pieces to a Man, which is generally the Fate of Foot that are interlin'd with Horfe when they are once routed, and efpecially when the other Foot are up with them.

Thus was the main Body of the Enemy, on which the Fate of the Day on both Sides depended, put to an entire Rout. The Veldt-Marfhal by this Time had routed their Right Wing, and drove them out of the Villages; moft of whom fled towards *Charleroy*. The Troops in *Ramillies* maintain'd that Poft with great Refolution, till they faw their main Body drove out of the Field; at which Time they quitted the Village, and made towards their Left Wing; but as they could not get out but in great Diforder, our Horfe fell in with 'em, and cut moft of them to Pieces.

Their Left Wing and the Front Line of our Right, where our Regiment was, ftood looking on all the while without ftriking a Stroke.

When the Elector and *Villeroy* faw they muft yield to Fate, they made the beft of their Way towards *Louvain*, picking up all the Stragglers they could by the Way, and fent them to their Left Wing; but the Duke purfued them clofe with the Horfe, leaving Orders for the Foot to follow as faft as poffible. The Foot continu'd marching till about One

1706. in the Morning; and after a Halt of near two Hours began our March again. The Duke purfued fo clofe that he got between their Left Wing and *Lovain*, which made them difperfe throughout their whole Country. The Elector and *Villeroy* finding they could make nothing of it at the *Dyle*, went on to *Villrood*, in Hopes of making a Stand at that Canal; but the Duke being clofe at their Heels, they made off from thence, and never look'd behind them till they got to *Lifle*.

The Duke halted with the Horfe at *Greenbury* for the Foot, who continued on a diforderly March, making as few Halts as poffible, till they came up with the Duke, where we halted till our Tents and Baggage came, and then march'd on to *Alofte*, and fo to *Ghent*.

Thus ended the famous Battle of *Ramillies*, in which the Duke of *Marlborough* acted the Part of a moft confummate General, not only in gaining fo great a Victory over the Enemy, who had fo great Advantage both in their Situation concerted, as well as Number of Troops; but alfo in purfuing the Advantage that accrued thereby: The Confequence of which was, the Conqueft of all the *Spanifh* Netherlands. Moreover, the demolifhing their old Lines, and taking the ftrong Fortrefs of *Menin*; in the Siege of which our Regiment was employ'd, when we paid for our looking on at *Ramillies*.

The Remarks I fhall make on this famous Battle is, to fhew our young Gentlemen that have never been in Action, the dangerous Confequence of a General breaking his Order of Battle; the Nature of which ought to be well weigh'd and confidered; efpecially when he is on the Defenfive, before the Enemy comes up with him. It was the Feint the Duke of *Marlborough* made with his Right Wing, that

made

of the Duke of Marlborough.

made them alter their Plan of Battle, which always 1706. occasions Disorder by so sudden and unexpected an Alteration; and one might imagine that the Elector and *Villeroy*, who had rode so often over those Grounds, should have known them better than the Duke of *Marlborough*, and not to have been thus amus'd by him.

The Intent of their interlining Foot with their Horse on the Plain, was to sustain the Horse in Case of a Repulse, under the Shelter of whose Fire they may easily rally again; for the Horse never care to come within the Fire of the Foot; wherefore the Duke was oblig'd to do the same; for in this Case they may be of great Use to the Horse: But then the Horse are to take great Care whenever they happen to break, that they ride not in upon the Front of their Foot; if they do, they will as surely fire upon them as they would upon the Enemy.

The Foot that are posted after this Manner, are to take great Care that they spend not all their Fire at once, lest the Enemy's Horse take that Opportunity of breaking in upon them, which the Foot will be too apt to do, unless the commanding Officer give the Officers of the Platoons great Caution of being very careful in observing such Orders as he shall give, on whom all their Behaviour depends; for in this Case there may be Occasion only to fire sometimes from the Right and sometimes from the Left, and half their Fire from either will be sufficient at once. The Foot that are posted after this Manner are in a dangerous Situation; if they lose the Day they are entirely cut to Pieces, not One in a Hundred escapes, nor can they possibly expect Quarter, in the Hurry and Confusion all are in at such a Juncture.

The Duke of *Marlboro*'s Conduct on his Pursuit is worthy Observation; how many Instances have we

70   MEMOIRS *of all the Campaigns*

1706. in History of great Victories being obtain'd, that have turned to little or no Advantage, for want of pursuing the Blow, while the Enemy were in a Pannick and Consternation?

As to the Loss on both Sides, I refer to the publick Papers; so shall say no more of the following Part of the Campaign, only that it was taken up in the Sieges of *Ostend*, *Menin*, and *Aeth*.

Antwerp and *Dendermond* stood a Blockade for some time; the Magistrates of all the rest of the Towns came to the Duke with their Keys, and made their Submission: so, after having demolish'd the Enemies old Lines, which had been the Barrier to *France* since their Conquest in the *Netherlands*, we in *October* went into Quarters.

1707. The ill Success of the Elector and *Villeroy* put old *Lewis* on sending the Duke of *Vendome* to command in their Stead; but with positive Orders not to hazard a Battle, unless it were in the Defence of their Lines, which were thrown up last Winter.

The most remarkable Thing in this Campaign was our dirty March to *Soniers*, which was as follows: The Duke being encamp'd at *Meldert* near *Louvain*, *Vendome* came out of his Lines, and encamp'd at *Gennep*, within four Leagues of us, but kept a watchful Eye on the Duke; who he knew would be for attacking him, if he should give him the least Opportunity: which was very true; for when the Duke found him encamp'd so very near, he lay very quiet for about a Month, till on the 30th of *June*, on beating Tattoo, the Duke decamp'd on a sudden, and sending away the heavy Baggage to *Louvain*, march'd all the Night towards *Vendome*; and by the time it was Day, had got the right Wing of Horse very near him; who at this time had just struck his Camp, and march'd off in great Hurry:

on

on which he order'd Count *Tilly* to advance with the Horse, and engage him till the Army came up, but the Country wherein *Vendome* was, being full of Inclosures, *Tilly* could not come at them for Want of the Foot, who were a great Way behind; so that they could not come time enough to his Assistance, by which *Vendome* march'd off at his Leisure. The Duke finding the Foot fatigued with their Night-March, order'd the Army to incamp, and the Horse to get Forrage; which *Vendome* perceiving, thought the Duke had given over his Design; therefore encamp'd at *Seneff*, two Leagues from us.

When the Duke found he halted so near him, as soon as it grew dark he march'd again towards him; but it now fell a raining to that degree, that our Men could hardly stand under it; however we made a Shift to get up with them by the time it was Day, which *Vendome* little expected, who immediately struck his Camp, and march'd off in great Confusion: but, as the Rain continued with Violence, so that the Infantry could neither keep their Arms dry, nor come up to assist the Cavalry, otherwise he would have paid for his halting at *Seneff*; he therefore made never another Halt till he got within his Lines at *Mons*, from whence he did not stir more this Campaign. The Duke finding the Enemy gone off, and the Rain continue, turned to the Right, and encamp'd at *Sonier*, and tho' it was not more than two Leagues from our former Ground, the Horse marching before the Foot, made the Ground so miry, that a great many Men perish'd in the Sloughs; and it was three Days before the last of our Foot got up. Our Army lay here Weather-bound a full Month before we could get hence; and as nothing of Consequence happen'd after, I end this Campaign.

1708. The *French* King finding he could do nothing in *Flanders*, resolv'd on trying what he could do with the *Pretender* in *Scotland*; the disaffected Party of that Kingdom having often sollicited him to send the *Pretender* to them, on which they would do Wonders: this put Old *Lewis* on fitting out a Squadron of 24 light Ships at *Dunkirk*, commanded by the Chevalier *Forbin*, who in the Beginning of *March* sail'd with the *Pretender* and a Body of Troops towards the *Firth* of *Edinburgh*.

England had timely Notice of their Design, and had order'd Sir *George Byng* with a good Squadron to watch *Forbin*'s Motion; however, could not prevent his sailing out of *Dunkirk*, and had got 18 Hours start of him: Sir *George* follow'd, keeping along the *English* Coast, *Forbin* having kept on the other Side the Channel along the Coast of *Holland*.

There was upon this Occasion 10 *British* Battalions from *Flanders* order'd to embark at *Ostend* on board Transports, and sail under Convoy of Admiral *Baker*, who had ten Men of War for that Purpose. We sail'd to *Tinmouth*, where we lay on board, waiting the Event of Sir *George*, who had by this time got near the Mouth of the *Firth*: But *Forbin* keeping on the opposite Shore, when he stood over, found he had overshot his Post, wherefore was forced to tack to recover it: but, as he was just upon standing in to the *Firth*, he perceived Sir *George*, upon which he tack'd again, and crouding all the Sail he could, stood away towards the Coast of *Denmark*; and having clear light Ships, out-sail'd Sir *George*, and got back to *Dunkirk*. Thus ended this famous Expedition, after which our ten Battalions sail'd back to *Ostend*, and landed the 14th of *April*.

In the Beginning of *May* the Duke assembled the Army at *Tarleank*, between *Louvain* and *Brussels*,

where

of the Duke of Marlborough. 73

where he waited for the coming of Prince *Eugene,* 1708.
who was on a full March from the *Rhine* with 30,000
Germans to join him.

Old *Lewis* having fail'd in his *Scottish* Expedition,
had now form'd another Project to be transacted in
the *Netherlands* this Campaign; wherefore he had augmented his Army to 110,000, with whom *Vendome*
encamp'd between *Soniers* and *Chirre:* Here the
Duke of *Burgundy* came, and took the Command of
the Army, who was accompany'd by the Duke of
Berry, and the *Pretender,* under the Title of the
Chevalier de St. George: On *Vendome*'s advancing
to *Soniers,* the Duke march'd to *Hall,* in order to
cover *Brussels,* on which he thought the Enemy had
a Design.

The Project that he thought had been concerted in
the Court of *France* for the Operations of this Campaign was this: The Elector of *Bavaria,* when
Governor of the Low Countries, had liv'd after
a most profuse Manner, which gained much on the
Affections of the People, especially among the Ladies, and still kept up a secret Correspondence among
them; and had now brought Matters to bear, that
the Magistrates of most of the Towns were to deliver
them up to the *French,* whenever their Army appeared before them.

My Lord *Marlboro'* (whose Intelligence in the
Court of *France* never fail'd him) had timely Notice of all this, wherefore it was that he had sent
to Prince *Eugene* to come to his Assistance. *Burgundy* had the Command of the *French* Army, yet
the Management was wholly in *Vendome*; so, according to the above Scheme, towards the latter End
of *June,* he decamp'd very silently, upon beating
Tattoo, and never halted till he came before the
Gates of *Ghent,* which the Magistrates threw open
to him, and receiv'd Lieut. Gen. *Lamott* with 20,000

Men,

Men, 5,000 of which he sent that Night to *Bruges*, which did the same.

Vendome puff'd with this Success, march'd next Morning to the *Scheld*, in hopes to get into *Oudenarde* after the same Manner; but my Lord *Marlboro'* was before-hand with him there: for, next Morning, after *Vendome* had stole this March of him, he decamp'd, and follow'd as fast as he could, and got to *Oudenarde* before him; upon which *Vendome* crossed the *Scheld* at *Gaver*, thinking to get home that Way. Upon the Duke's coming to *Oudenarde*, he order'd Bridges to be laid over the *Scheld*, a little below the Town, and the Foot to pass as they came up, while he at the Head of the Horse pass'd thro' the Town, and drew up between *Vendome* and home, who begun now to wish he had never undertook their fine Project, and was at a Loss what to do: to return to *Ghent*, was to be penn'd up in a Corner of the Country, and cut off from his Garrisons; and he knew the *Germans* would join the Duke in a few Days; he therefore resolved to stand a Battle; and tho' he was at least 10,000 Men stronger than the Duke, yet he would not venture to attack him, but drew up his Army behind a strong Piece of Ground, having the *Scheld* with a great many Inclosures on his left, with the Village *Greenheim* in the Front of the Inclosures, from whence was a marshy Ground full of Trees and Brush-Wood, which extended to a rising Ground, whereon was a noble Plain, on which he drew up all his Cavalry interlined with some Foot: Behind the marshy Ground, and so on to the *Scheld*, he drew up all the rest of his Infantry, and placed in the Village some Foot and Dragoons; he also caus'd a great many Trees to be cut down in the marshy Ground, to obstruct our Passage.

of the Duke of Marlborough.

This was the Difpofition *Vendome* had made of his 1708.
Army.

The Duke ranged the greateft Part of his Infantry from the *Scheld*, along the marfhy Ground; and in the Plain drew up all the Cavalry, keeping with him 15 Battalions of the *Dutch* Foot under the Command of the Prince of *Orange*. Before the Duke had form'd his Lines, Prince *Eugene* came up in Perfon, but had left his Troops two Days March behind.

The Battle began by attacking the Village near the *Scheld*, which being advanced fomething from their Line, they quitted with little Oppofition; upon which our Infantry acted on the marfhy Grounds, and attack'd their main Body of Foot, who ftood their Ground with great Refolution; at the fame time our Cavalry on the Plain advanc'd on theirs with fuch Refolution, as made them give Way at once: nor did they make one brave Charge all this Day, but ftill gave Ground as our Horfe charged them. Our Infantry here engaged theirs; fo that they gave no Difturbance to our Horfe, who alfo fhrunk back with their Horfe: thus we kept preffing on them in the Plain till we drove them paft the marfhy Ground, they never making one gallant Pufh all this While: at length our Horfe drove refolutely in upon them, which entirely broke them, and put them to the Rout; nor could all their Generals get them to rally again, fo as to give the leaft Affiftance in helping to bring off their Foot, thofe of their Foot in the Plain undergoing the Fate that attend all Foot in the like Cafe.

Their Infantry that defended the marfhy Ground behaved very gallantly, infomuch that our Foot could not force them from thence, till the Prince of *Orange* came on their Flank with the 13 *Dutch* Battalions he
had

had with him; and they seeing their Horse drove out of the Field, made down to the Inclosures on the *Scheld*, where our Horse could not come at them, nor could the Foot follow them, being very much fatigued; however, they pour'd their Fire in upon them as they were going off, which did great Execution.

Vendome with his shater'd Troops made the best of his Way to *Ghent*, nor did he think himself safe till he had got thorough the Town, and encamp'd along the Canal to *Bruges*. There were kill'd and taken of the Enemy about 10,000; and were it not for the Inclosures along the *Scheld*, hardly any of their Foot would have got off.

Our Foot suffer'd most on this Occasion; nor did the Duke pursue them much further than the Field of Battle, on which we lay all Night.

Next Day a Detachment was sent to secure the Enemies Lines at *Warneston*. The *Germans* being arriv'd, our Generals resolv'd on the Siege of *Lisle*; a bold Undertaking: Whereupon we marched, and invested that famous City: However, the Marshal *Boufflers* found Means to throw himself with a good Body of Troops into it; so that the Garrison consisted of 14,000 effective Men, besides a great Number of the Inhabitants, who did good Service during the Siege. The Out-Works and Fortifications, together with the Citadel, were *Vaubon*'s Master-Piece, whereon he had exerted the utmost of his Skill, and was said to be a hazardous Undertaking of our Generals.

The second of *August*, O. S. our Army sate down before *Lisle*; Prince *Eugene* undertook the Siege with 50 Battalions and 40 Squadrons (our Regiment being one, wherein we suffer'd very much) while the Duke

of the Duke of Marlborough. 77

Duke of *Marlboro'* with the rest of the Army co-ver'd him.

1708.

The *French* Court, who expected great Matters from this Campaign, were very much surpriz'd and chagrin'd on the Defeat of their Army at *Oudenard*; but were Thunder-struck when they found their Lines demolish'd, and their beloved City of *Lisle* invested: Whereupon they immediately ordered the Duke of *Berwick* to march with a strong Detachment from the *Rhine* to the *Netherlands* to assist *Vendome* in raising the Siege. *Berwick* came, and encamp'd between *Doway* and *Tournay*, to cover that Part of the Country from our Parties.

I shall take no Notice of the Progress of this famous Siege, more than the Stratagems used by the Generals on both Sides; the one for carrying it on, and the other for raising it. *Vendome* lay encamp'd on the Canal (from whence the Princes of the Blood, with the *Chevalier*, went home by the Way of *Newport*) till the Arrival of the Duke of *Berwick*, at which time he march'd thro' *Ghent*, and keeping the *Scheld* on his Right, marched up that River, till he came near *Tournay*, where he cross'd it, and join'd *Berwick*: and now being much superior in Numbers, gave out, that he would oblige our Generals to raise the Siege; whereupon he advanc'd towards the Duke, upon which Prince *Eugene* came and join'd him with what Troops could be spared from the Siege, leaving the Prince of *Orange* to command in his Absence. *Vendome* advanc'd within Cannon-shot of the Duke, and fell to cannonading each other with great Fury for the whole Day after; on which he retired at a small Distance: upon which the Duke caused an Intrenchment to be thrown up in the Front of his Camp, to prevent any sudden Surprize, and Prince *Eugene* returned again to the Siege. In a few

Days

1708. Days after, *Vendome* advanced a second time, which brought Prince *Eugene* again from the Siege, and both Armies fell again to cannonading, which continued till Night; when they lay on their Arms till Morning, at which time our General expected to be attack'd, but they fell to cannonading again. Our Generals finding this wasted their Ammunition much, and that our Men were pretty well cover'd by the Intrenchment from their Fire, therefore grew sparing of it. This *Vendome* very well knew therefore, when we abated in our Fire, and that it would be too hazardous to attack us: besides, he found no Ardor in his Troops to it; he therefore formed a Design for cutting off our Communication from our Garrisons on the other Side the *Scheld*, from whence we had all our Stores and Provisions; he therefore drew off in the Night, and marched to the other Side of the *Scheld*, and ranged his Army along the Banks of that River, and threw up a strong Intrenchment all the Way to *Oudenard*, carrying it round the Town by *Gaver*; by which he effected his Design, and was confident our Army could not subsist long before *Lisle*: but the Duke foreseeing the Difficulties that would arise from thence, had sent an Express to *England* for Lieut. Gen. *Earl*, who at this time was embark'd with 6000 Men for *Spain*, and lay Wind-bound, to sail to *Ostend*: so the Wind that prevented his sailing to *Spain*, brought him to *Ostend*, with a great Quantity of Stores and Provisions; as also great Quantities sent from *Holland*; from whence he sent, soon after his Arrival, a large Convoy of all manner of Necessaries, which were much wanted at the Siege: On which the Duke march'd with the Covering-Army to *Rosilare*, to facilitate the Convoys that were to come from *Ostend*, whence he sent Major-Gen. *Webb* with 6000 Men to bring up
this

of the Duke of Marlborough.

this firſt Convoy. *Vendome* ſaw that the Fate of 1708.
Liſle depended in a great meaſure on its Arrival;
wherefore he ordered Lieut. Gen. *Lamott* to march
with 24,000 Men to intercept it. *Lamott* came up
with *Webb* at the Wood of *Winnendale,* who drew
up his Men to all the Advantage the Ground would
admit of. *Lamott* fell to cannonading him, but
Webb ordered his Men to lie flat on the Ground;
by which the Cannon did little, or no Hurt: after
this *Lamott* attack'd him ſeveral times, and was as
often repuls'd.

The Duke having an Account of the March of
Lamott, ordered Lieut. Gen. *Cadogan* with a Body
of Horſe to the Succour of *Webb*; who, upon the
hearing *Lamott*'s Cannon, made all the Haſte he
could to *Webb*'s Aſſiſtance; on whoſe appearing *Lamott*
left the Field with great Precipitation, leaving
all his Cannon; and this grand Convoy arrived ſafe,
which may be ſaid was the taking of *Liſle.* *Webb*
gain'd great Honour by this gallant Action, tho' a
great deal was owing to *Lamott*'s ill Conduct; and
Webb ſpoil'd all, by boaſting too much of it.

Boufflers having been too profuſe of his Ammunition
at the Beginning of the Siege, began now to
want Powder; who found Means to acquaint *Vendome,*
who could find no other Way of ſupplying
him, but by ordering the Duke of *Luxemberg* with
2000 choice Horſe, each of them taking 100 lb.
of Powder behind him, and ſo to make a bold Puſh
for throwing themſelves into *Liſle*: whereupon they
advanced with great Boughs in their Hats along the
Cauſeway that leads from *Doway*; and marching in
great Order up to our advanc'd Guard, who, upon
challenging them, anſwered, they were *Germans* of
our Army, that had been on an Out-Command, and
were returning with Priſoners they had taken; upon
which

1708. which the Officer let them pass: but coming to the next Guard, the Officer examining them more strictly, they then clapp'd Spurs to their Horses, and rode by the Guard as hard as they could drive towards the Town; but the Officer firing on them, gave the Alarm; so all that were in their Way turn'd out, and fell firing at them, killing a good many of them, and setting Fire to their Baggs of Powder; however, the foremost drove on, so that near 1000 'of them got into the Town in a Cloud of Smoak; for riding in a Crowd, the Baggs which our Men had set Fire to, set Fire to others, by which a great many were blown up; those that were behind made backwards to *Doway*: but a great many were kill'd before they got clear of our Camp. This Affair happened the very Day of *Winnendal* Fight.

There came two other Convoys safe from *Ostend*, which did the Business, and that was all; for soon after *Vendome* found Means to cut off our Communication with *Ostend*, by taking the Post of *Leffingen*, and then cutting the Dykes, laid all that Country under Water: but this was too late, for *Boufflers* was, on the 12th of *October*, obliged to surrender the Town, and retire with his Garrison into the Citadel, having not above 5000 fit for Service.

About this time the Elector of *Bavaria* with 12,000 Men came before *Brussels*, expecting that the Inhabitants would rise in his Favour: but tho' their Inclinations were good, yet seeing how Matters went, kept them quiet; and Count *Pascal* the Governor, with a Garrison of 5000 Men, behaved with great Bravery. The Elector made a Lodgment on the Counterscarp, and a Breach in the Wall; but by a vigorous Sally of the Garrison, he was drove from the Counterscarp with a considerable Loss. The Duke hearing the Elector was sate down before *Brussels*,

of the Duke of Marlborough.

sels, resolved on the Relief of it; therefore marched towards the *Scheld*, leaving Prince *Eugene* in Possession of the Town of *Lisle*, to carry on the Siege of the Citadel.

Upon the Duke's approaching the *Scheld*, he made two Detachments, one under the Command of the Earl of *Orkney*, and Count *Loatain*; the other under Lieut. Gen. *Cadogan* and Brigadier *Evans*: the former march'd to *Gaver*, the latter to *Kirkhoven*, where they both pass'd the *Scheld*, without the least Opposition, to the great Shame of the Arms of *France*, and Surprize of all Men; upon which the *French* abandon'd all their mighty Works they had thrown up along that River, some making towards *Tournay*, but the greatest Part towards *Ghent*, leaving most of their Cannon behind them. The Duke march'd with the Main of his Army to *Kirkhoven*, where having pass'd the *Scheld*, he march'd to *Brussels*; but, on the Elector's hearing he had pass'd the *Scheld*, he stole off in the Night, and made the best of his Way to *Namur*, leaving all his Cannon, Ammunition, and Wounded behind him. Soon after this *Boufflers* surrendred the Citadel of *Lisle*, and *Vendome* march'd home by the Way of *Newport*, leaving *Lamott* with about 20,000 Men to defend his new Conquest of *Ghent* and *Bruges*: but the Duke dislodg'd him from thence before he put the Army into Quarters; for he sate down before *Ghent* on the 7th of *December*, and on the 24th *Lamott* surrendred, having Liberty to march home after *Vendome* with all his Troops. Thus ended this great and long Campaign, with Disgrace and Mortification to the *French* Court.

1708.

This was a very wet Spring, our Army could not take the Field till the latter End of *May*. The Duke open'd the Campaign near *Mennin*, where Prince *Eugene*

1709

F

1709. Eugene join'd him with his *Germans*, our Army being upwards of 100,000, advanced to the other Side of *Lisle*.

The *French* King being displeased with the Conduct of the Duke of *Vendome*, sent this Year the Marshal *Villars* to command in his Stead, who drew his Army together at *Pont a Vendine*, within the new Lines they had thrown up last Winter. Our Generals advanced and encamp'd within less than two Leagues of him, and rode out next Morning to take a View of his Situation, which made him believe they design'd to attack him in that Post; wherefore he sent immediately to *Tournay* and *Doway* for a great Part of the Troops that garrison'd those Places, to join him.

Upon our beating Tattoo this Evening, Orders came along the Line for us to strike our Tents, and march. This made us believe that our Generals did really design to attack their Lines next Morning; but on our marching off to the Left, which was quite the contrary Way, we could not tell what to think of it; yet, when Day appear'd, were not a little surprized to find ourselves before the City of *Tournay*, which we immediately invested. This was no less a Surprize on *Villars*, especially since he had drain'd the City of the best of its Troops, there being not above 5000 Men left to defend the great Number of Works that were about it; nor was it now in the Power of *Villars* to return those Troops.

SIEGE of TOURNAY.

This was a nice Finesse of our Generals, worthy a Remark. The *French* Court was surprized when they heard of it, wherefore they sent Marshal *Boufflers* with a Reinforcement of Troops from the *Rhine*, to
join

of the Duke of Marlborough. 83

join *Villars*, by which his Army was 15000 more 1709.
than ours. I shall not take Notice of the Progress
of the Siege, more than that Prince *Eugene* undertook
it, while the Duke cover'd him; (our Regiment,
tho' employ'd in the Siege of both the Town
and Citadel of *Lisle*, was also at the Siege of both
Town and Citadel of this Place, and were great Sufferers
at both.) The Marquis *De Surville*, who commanded,
surrendred the Town on the 19th of *July*,
and retired into the Citadel; which is certainly one
of the best fortify'd Places by Art that is in the
World, there being more Works a great deal under
Ground than above, which made our Approach very
difficult; insomuch that we were obliged to carry
great Part of our Works under Ground, by which,
and the springing their Mines, we lost great Numbers
of Men: However, they having but a slender
Garrison, their Men were fatigued out of their
Lives, so were obliged to surrender on the 22d of
August.

This important Place being taken, our Generals
design'd on *Mons*; in order to which the Prince
of *Hesse* was sent with a strong Detachment before
to dislodge a Party of Dragoons that were posted
near *Mons*, the Army marching soon after him; but,
upon the Approach of the Prince, the Dragoons drew
off - - - - When *Villars* found *Tournay* invested, he
pass'd the *Scharp*, and encamp'd between that River
and the *Scheld*, and marched that Way, in hopes of
getting thither before them: but finding they had
got before him, he stopp'd short at *Malplacquet*, and
finding it a strong Situation, resolved upon maintaining
that Post, in order to give what Disturbance he
could in our carrying on the Siege: whereupon he
immediately fell to work in throwing up a strong Intrenchment,
and cutting down Trees in the Wood

that cover'd him, laying them acrofs to prevent our coming at him.

Our Generals finding *Villars* poffeffed of this Ground, refolved to diflodge him: they march'd up to him the fame Afternoon, and after taking a View of his Situation, were for attacking him at once; but, as our Right Wing and fome Battalions that were left to level the Works of *Tournay*, were not yet come, and the Day far fpent, they deferr'd it till Morning: however, both Armies cannonaded each other with great Fury, and *Villars* kept his Men at Work all Night; fo that in the Morning his Army feemed to be drawn up within a ftrong Fortification. His Right was cover'd with a Morafs with Intrenchments and Hedges before him; in his Left he had the Wood of *Sart*, and along his Front were feveral Woods interfperfed with Trees cut down, and Intrenchments thrown up one within another; infomuch that it was generally believed our Generals would not venture to attack them; and efpecially fince they could carry on the Siege of *Mons* without coming to that Extremity: but wanton with Succefs, our Troops come up, on the 31ft of *Auguft*, O. S. and the Attack was made about half an Hour after Eight in the Morning. General *Schulemberg*, with the *Germans* on the Right, attack'd the Left of the Enemy in the Wood of *Sart*; the Duke of *Argyll*, with Part of the *Britifh* Troops, attack'd the Intrenchments about *Tanniers*. Lieut. Gen. *Withers*, with the Right of the *Britifh* and Auxiliaries, attack'd thofe about *Blarengiers* and *Malplacquet*; and the Prince of *Orange* at the Head of the *Dutch* attack'd their Right, and thofe in the Wood of *Lamert*.

Thus was *Villars* attack'd by our Infantry in all Parts at once, our Cavalry drawn up clofe in the Rear, till our Infantry, after a long and bloody Difpute,

of the Duke of Marlborough. 85

pute, broke in upon them in all Places, and put 'em to the Rout; at which time the Cavalry fell on them, and made a moſt terrible Slaughter: however, tho' *Villars* behaved with great Courage and Reſolution, and was carry'd wounded out of the Field, yet *Boufflers* made a gallant Retreat towards *Queſnoy*, and drew within their Lines that were between that Place and *Valenchinis*. Our Generals had enough of this Battle; for they did not offer to purſue, after we had drove them a little Way from their Works, but reſted ſatisfy'd with being Maſters of the Field. It was the moſt deſperate and bloody Attack and Battle that had been fought in the Memory of Man; and both our Generals were very much blam'd for throwing away ſo many brave Men's Lives, when there was no Occaſion: It was the only raſh Thing the Duke of *Marlboro'* was ever guilty of; and it was generally believ'd that he was preſs'd to it by Prince *Eugene:* and this very Battle gave the Duke's Enemies a Handle to exclaim againſt him, in ſaying he was a Man delighted in War, and valued not the Lives of Men.

1709.

The Battle laſted from Eight in the Morning till Three in the Afternoon. The Loſs was computed to be near 18,000 kill'd and wounded on each Side; but we took a great many Priſoners, with all their Artillery. After the Battle we inveſted *Mons*, which ſurrendred the 9th of *October*, and then both Armies went into Quarters.

Our two Generals, reſolved to puſh on the War in theſe Parts, aſſembled the Army near *Tournay*, in the Beginning of *April*, before the *French* could get into the Field; by which we paſs'd their Lines, on the 9th, at *Pont a Vendin*, without the leaſt Oppoſition, from whence we march'd to the Plains of *Lens*.

1710.

F 3 *Villars*

1710. *Villars* at this time was affembling his Army behind the *Scharp*; but on our advancing towards him, he retired with Precipitation behind the *Senfett*, leaving fome of his Tents and Baggage behind him: on which we invefted *Doway*, in which and Fort *Scharp* were a Garrifon of 1000 Men, commanded by Lieut. Gen. *Albergotty*, an old experienced Officer.

Soon after *Doway* was invefted, *Villars* having got all his Army together, drew from behind the *Senfett*, and encamp'd on the Plains before *Arrafs*; and, according to the *French* Way of Gafconading, gave out, that he would make our Generals repent their fitting down before *Doway*: upon which the Duke drew the Covering-Army on the Plains before *Doway*, and made a Difpofition for receiving him, whilft Prince *Eugene* was carrying on the Siege.

Villars advanc'd within Cannon-fhot of us, and made a Shew of attacking us, on which Prince *Eugene* join'd us with what Troops could be fpared from the Siege; but they foon found this was only a *French* Air of *Villars* to retard the Siege: whereupon the Duke order'd a flight Intrenchment to be thrown up in the Front of his Camp, and Prince *Eugene* return'd to the Siege, and *Villars* march'd back to the Plains of *Arrafs*. Notwithftanding *Albergotty* made a very gallant Defence in difputing every Inch of Ground, and making feveral defperate Sallies, in which great Numbers were kill'd on both Sides; yet he was obliged to furrender both the Town and Fort *Scharp*, on the 15th of *June*. This Siege was no fooner over, tho' *Villars*'s Army much out-number'd ours, than he retir'd behind the *Senfett*, fo that there was no coming at him, nor laying Siege to *Arrafs*: on which our Generals laid Siege to *Bethune*, which furrendred the 20th of *Auguft*. After which we invefted

of the Duke of Marlborough.

vested both *St. Vincent* and *Arre* at the same time. 1710. The first of these Places surrendred in a short time; but *Arre*, very strong by Art and Nature, held out a long Siege, and did not surrender till the latter End of *October*; *Villars* all the while never offering to stir from behind the *Senset*. This Siege over, both Armies went into Quarters.

I am now come to the last Campaign the Duke 1711. of *Marlboro'* ever made. Our Affairs in *England* having taken another Turn, the Queen, soon after the Death of her Bosom-Friend, the Prince of *Denmark*, was so infatuated as to change her old trusty Ministry, and brought in a Sett of vile Creatures, that were entirely in the *Pretender*'s Interest, who overturn'd all that had hitherto been doing; and tho' *France* was reduced to the last Extremity, and not able to hold out another Campaign, yet did these perfidious Men prevail so far on this weak Woman, the Queen, as to court *France* for a Peace, in order to bring in their beloved *Chevalier*: But this being foreign to my Purpose, I shall wave that Matter, and return to our Campaign. In order to which, the Duke of *Marlboro'* shew'd some of the finest Schemes and Turns in War, that is to be found in History; therefore I shall be the more particular in relating it according to the best of my Judgment and Knowledge.

The Beginning of *May* our Army rendezvous'd near *Doway*, where both our Generals came to the Head of us; but our Cabinet-General at Home, and the Court of *France*, had so concerted Matters, that broke all the Measures our Generals had taken for putting an End to the War this Campaign; for *France*, instead of sending a powerful Army into the *Netherlands*, to withstand our two Generals, order'd only between 80 and 90,000 under *Villars* to guard the new

1711. new Lines they had thrown up laſt Winter, having ſent all the Forces they could ſpare to the *Rhine* from all Parts, in order to ſend the Elector of *Bavaria* with a Body of Troops into his own Country; as alſo for diſturbing the Election of the preſent Emperor *Charles* the Sixth, which was to be held at *Francfort* this Summer. This oblig'd Prince *Eugene* to march with his Troops with what Expedition he could to the *Rhine*; and our Miniſtry, to prevent the Duke from doing any thing againſt *Villars*, ſent for about 6000 of our *Britiſh* Troops to go upon their famous *Canada* Expedition; ſo that my Lord *Marlborough* was left alone with an Army not quite 75,000, and notwithſtanding *Villars* was more than 10,000 more than the Duke, yet he had poſitive Orders from his Court not to hazard a Battle, unleſs it were in Defence of his Lines, which was now the laſt Barrier *France* had on their Side to cover their Country; for old *Lewis*, at this Time, having coin'd a new Army of *French* Guineas, fought his Battles with much more Succeſs in our Cabinet, than his Army could do in the Field; wherefore all that *Villars* could do was to keep the Duke of *Marlborough* out of his Lines, which conſidering the Strength and Nature of them, one might imagine was no great Hardſhip upon him, for they were the ſtrongeſt that ever *France* had, being juſt on the very Brink of the Kingdom.

Soon after Prince *Eugene* march'd off, the Duke advanc'd into the Plains of *Lens*, having his Left within half a League of *Doway*, in Hopes it might tempt *Villars* to draw out of his Lines, and give him Battle on theſe Plains; but *Villars* took Care to obſerve his Orders, and would not ſtir a Foot from thence, whereupon the Duke form'd one of the nobleſt

of the Duke of Marlborough. 89

bleft Schemes that ever was projected by a General, 1711.
which was as follows.

That Part of *Villars*'s Lines wherein he lay encamp'd, had a large deep Morafs in the Front of them, near an *English* Mile over, which was occafion'd by the *Senfett* branching out in feveral Channels from *Arrafs*, which made this Morafs extend all the Way from thence to *Boufhain*, over which were two Caufeways, for the Conveniency of the Country People. *Villars* had thefe in his Front, and on our Side of one of 'em was a ftrong Fort call'd *Arleux*, in which he kept a ftrong Garrifon. The Duke wanted to have *Villars* himfelf demolifh this Fort. He faw he could take it when he pleas'd, and demolifh it when he had done, but he knew as foon as he was march'd from thence, *Villars* would foon come and rebuild it; but fhould he pretend to fortify it, then he expected as foon as he was march'd off, *Villars* would come and retake and demolifh it. According to this Scheme the Duke made a Detachment of as many Battalions and Squadrons as were requifite for that Purpofe, under the Command of Lieutenant-General *Rantzaw*, an old experienc'd Officer; and order'd that this Detachment fhould incamp on the Glacis of *Doway*, two fmall Leagues from *Arleux*, there to lie till Matters were got ready for the Siege. The Lieutenant-General thinking the Detachment fafe under the Cannon of *Doway*, took up his Quarters in Town, as did alfo the commanding Officers; and thofe that lay in Camp took Example of their Commanders, and thinking themfelves fecure, were not troubled about keeping fuch Out-Guards as were neceffary.

Villars having an Account of the carelefs Encampment of this Detachment, fent a good Body of Horfe and Dragoons over the Caufey of *Arleux*, and
from

from thence when it grew duskish march'd with all the Silence imaginable towards our Detachment, so that about One in the Morning he took them Napping, without being challeng'd by one Centinel, fell in upon the right Flank of the Horse, where they made great Havock; but the Quarter-Guards of the Foot, taking the Alarm, fired at them: This alarm'd the Foot, who running to Arms even in their Shirts, attack'd them with the greatest Fury, and put a Stop to their advancing any further than the Horse; but had they not fallen to plunder as they did (a bewitching Thing to all Soldiers, whereby many a Battle has been lost, and brave Designs frustrated) they might have cut the whole Detachment to Pieces, and have had the Plunder when they had done. *Villars* finding the Foot had got to their Arms, order'd his Men to retire, who did with little or no Loss to themselves, but had kill'd and wounded a great many of our Troopers, and carried off most of their Horses.

This was the only Affront the Duke of *Marlborough* receiv'd during the whole War, nor indeed could the Blame be imputed to him. However, this may be a Caution to all Officers from the General to the Subaltern, never to think themselves too secure, let the Command be what it will; for could any Thing seem more so, than this Detachment, that was under the Cannon of such a fortified Town as *Doway*, and our grand Army incamp'd so near them? which makes good the old Proverb, *Security dwells next Door to Ruin.*

The Duke was not a little ruffled on this Occasion, nor was *Villars* less elated, or the *Paris* Gazettes wanting in magnifying the Thing, and sounding the Praise of *Villars*.——However, this Mouthful of Moon-shine did not last long. In a few Days after the Duke order'd the same Detachment to march and

lay

of the Duke of Marlborough.

lay Siege to *Arleux*, who made themselves Masters 1711. of it in about eight Days. *Villars* with the whole *French* Army, then within a Mile of 'em, stood looking on this Fort being taken. The Duke seem'd very intent in having the Breaches repair'd, and new Works added to it, and appointed Engineers to see those Things done. However, in a few Days after, the Duke leaving but a slender Garrison therein, yet made a Shew of repairing the old and going on with the new Works. He march'd the Army fifteen Leagues on a Stretch away to the Right, pitching his Camp at *Coat* near *Hesden*, and gave Orders to the Army to lay in good store of Forage; but we were no sooner sat down in this Camp, but an Express came from the Governor of *Arleux*, that *Villars* had besieged him; and as the Breaches were not repair'd, nor any thing done for strengthning it, he must be obliged to surrender, unless he was soon relieved. On which, the Duke order'd Lieutenant General *Cadogan* to march with forty Squadrons, and all the Grenadiers of the Army, to the Relief of *Arleux*; but by the Time *Cadogan* got to *Lens*, he had an Account that *Arleux* was taken, and that the Enemy were hard at Work in demolishing it. Thus far the Duke succeeded in his Scheme; but on the Return of *Cadogan*, he seem'd very much chagrin'd, and said he would be revenged on *Villars*, and attack him in his Lines. By this Time, *Villars* having attended the Duke in his March hither, was encamp'd between the Head of the *Senset* and *Hesden*, where there was neither River nor Morass, but a plain champaign Country; but then the Lines were prodigious strong, with a double Fauffee before them: And *Villars* hearing that the Duke resolved to attack him, made all the Preparations he could for giving him a warm Reception. He not only drained the Garrisons of *Arras* and *Cambray*, of whatever Men could be spared, but he also drew all the Troops that were in the Lines far and near to join him; and being puffed with his late Success, wrote to his Master to let him know, that he had now brought the Duke of *Marlborough* to his *Ne plus ultra*, which was the Duke's Motto.

In the mean Time, the Duke seem'd very peevish, and would see but little Company, and seemingly resolved upon attacking *Villars*. In order to which, he drew off the heavy Baggage, with four Battalions and twelve Squadrons, to take Care of it, and to march towards *Doway*. Two Days after, he sent off all the heavy Train with more Battalions and Squadrons, and the Day following he sent off all the Train (to four of the lightest Field Pieces) with all the Lumber of the Camp, and more Battalions and Squadrons, not leaving so much as a Coach or Chaise for himself or any General Officer. In this flying Condition he next Day march'd the Army to *Villerbrulen*, within a short League of *Villars*, who was now satisfied that the Duke was in earnest; for we had no sooner arrived at their Camp, but the Duke gave Orders for the Horse and Dragoons to cut Fascines. Early next Morning, being the twelfth of *July*, O. S. the Duke and most of the General Officers rode out at the Head of eighty Squadrons and all the Grenadiers of the Army, to take a View of the Lines and of *Villars*'s Situation.

Brigadier *Durell* commanded our *British* Grenadiers, of whom I desired Liberty to ride out with the Duke, who readily consented. The Duke, with a Crowd about him, rode as near the Lines as their Cannon would permit; along which he rode a League and half, having a fair View of them, and the Nature of the Ground before them. He often stopt, and

of the Duke of Marlborough. 93

and shew'd the General Officers how he would have 1711.
the Army drawn up before Day next Morning, and
pointing with his Cane to the several Places the Attacks should be made. This he spake openly in the
hearing of all about him, and as it were with a Confidence of Success; when at the same Time, every
one with him were surprized at this rash and dangerous Undertaking, and believed it proceeded from the
Affront *Villars* had put upon him, and the ill Treatment he had of late received from the Queen and her
Ministry, which had now made him desperate. After
he had made his Observations, and given such Orders
as he thought fit, he return'd to Camp, and gave
Orders for the Army to prepare for Battle.

The Duke was no sooner return'd to Camp, but
Cadogan slipt privately away, taking with him only
forty *Hussars*; and now both Armies were full of the
Event of the next Day. The Enemy long'd for its
coming, that they might have some Satisfaction for
the many Affronts they had received. On the
other Hand, Things on our Side had a quite different Effect; we knew our Artillery was gone off, the
Army weaken'd by several Detachments sent with it,
and the Enemy reinforced, so that they were double
our Number. Yet for all this, we still had Hopes
that the Duke had something more in his Head than
we could penetrate into. At length Tattoo beats,
and before it had done, Orders came along the Line,
to strike our Tents immediately, and in less than half
an hour, the whole Army was on their March to the
Left. This surprized us all, nor could any of the
Generals imagine the Design of it.

We continued our March all the Night, favour'd
with a full Moon and fair Weather. About Break
of Day, the Duke received an Express from *Cadogan*, that he and Lieutenant-General *Hompesch*, Go-

vernor

1711. vernor of *Doway*, had, a little before One o' Clock, pafs'd the Caufey of *Arleux* without Oppofition, and were actually in Poffeffion of the Enemies Lines; upon which, the Duke, who kept at the Head of our March, expecting the Event, rode off with all the Horfe and Dragoons of the Left Wing; fending Orders to every particular Regiment, to continue their March with all the Expedition they poffibly could. This was furprizing indeed, a Thing none ever dream'd of. When *Villars*'s Spies brought him an Account of our Army being on their March to the Left, he believed it to be a Feint of the Duke's to draw him off from the Poft he was in, fo that he did not ftir from thence till he had an Account of *Cadogan*'s paffing the Lines at *Arleux*. This was no lefs a Surprize to the Marfhal, than it was to us; it put him beyond his Reafon, he immediately put the Army on their March, while he with only one Hundred choice Dragoons, rode off like a Man diftracted, to fee how Matters were at *Arleux*. Thus he rode, without any Confideration, till he fell in with *Cadogan*'s advanced Guards, not knowing where he was, till he perceived them furrounding him; and having now no other Way to efcape being taken, he order'd the Dragoons to throw themfelves into the Ruins of an old Caftle that was at Hand, while he with only two more, rode thro' an Opening of our Horfe, who not minding him, follow'd the Crowd, by which he efcaped; but the Dragoons were all made Prifoners without firing a Shot.

Our Army continued marching with all the Expedition we poffibly could, every Regiment making the beft of their Way, without minding their Order of March, or waiting for thofe that fainted, or dropt behind. The Enemy did the fame; fo that it was a perfect Race between both Armies, in trying who
fhould

of the Duke of Marlborough.

should come first up with *Cadogan*; but as we had 1711. the Start, so we kept a Head of them, though they had the shorter Cut. When we came on the Plains before *Arrass*, our Foot march'd within View of the foremost of their Horse, and sometimes within a Mile of each other; and nothing could prevent our coming to Blows, but the *Scharp* which we past at *Victry*, the *Senset*, and Morass, that was now between us; and as we kept a Head of them, so we join'd *Cadogan* before they could come up to disturb him. But more than one half of our Foot dropt behind; nor did they all come up till two Days after; several fainted and died by the Way: But as our Right Wing of Horse brought up the Rear, so the Duke sent them Orders to see all the Foot before them. This was a March full 13 Leagues.

Now the Manner of *Cadogan*'s passing the Lines is as follows. The Duke having carried on his Scheme as above, to his reconnoitring the Lines, and *Cadogan*'s slipping out of the Camp, who made all the Haste he could to *Doway*, where he arrived a little after Ten at Night, and found Lieutenant-General *Hompesch*, on the Plain before the Town, at the Head of 22 Battalions and 40 Squadrons (who were mostly the Troops the Duke sent off, under Pretence of guarding the Lumber of the Camp) whereupon they march'd directly to *Arleux*; where there being none to oppose them, they laid Planks, and repair'd such Places of the Causey as *Villars* caused to be broke down, upon his marching from thence, and so entered the Lines. Thus was this noble Scheme as well executed as projected, which was entirely the Duke's own framing, and let none into the Secret, but the Field Deputies, Prince *Anhault* the *Prussian* General, *Cadogan*, and *Hompesch*. He had also contrived Matters so, as to have the Advantage of a full Moon

and

and a fine Night. *Cadogan* would have found it a difficult Task to repair, and the Army to pass the Causey in a dark Night. Providence seem'd to favour the Design.

Next Morning, the 14th, we found *Villars* with his Army drawn up in Order of Battle, about half a League in our Front, with his Right towards the Works of *Cambray*, his Left cover'd by a Morass, and along his Front were several deep hollow Ways. Our Army lay here on their Arms three Nights, waiting for the coming up of the last of our Men; *Villars* not in the least offering to disturb us, but seem'd satisfy'd in stopping us here; for we could not advance, without forcing him to a Battle to very great Disadvantage: nor could we move to the Right, for the Garrison of *Arras*, which would be too great an Undertaking, considering the Difficulties that would attend the besieging it: and on our Left lay the River *Scheld*, about a League and half from us, which being deep and ouzy, was dangerous to pass in the Face of so numerous an Army; and to return would be altogether as dangerous, besides the Disgrace. Whereupon the Duke's Enemies in the Army, who became Creatures of the Ministry, began to arraign his Conduct in not considering these Difficulties, particularly the Lord *North*, tho' in our passing the Lines, run out mightily in Praise of the Duke; but now he, and others of our Time-serving Gentlemen, began to rail heavily against the Duke. But my Lord *Marlboro'* soon stopp'd their Mouths, and convinc'd them, that he had not only consider'd all their suppos'd Difficulties that should arise upon this Occasion; but that he had carry'd his Scheme so far, as to the securing a Post in this important Pass into *France*; whereupon the Day after all our Army had got over the Pass, he march'd in Order of Battle at Noon-

of the Duke of Marlborough. 97

Noon-Day over a fine Plain towards the *Scheld*, along 1711. the Front of *Villars*'s Army, who now and then saluted us with a Cannon, as our Army came to the *Scheld*. The Duke drew them up facing *Villars*'s Right Wing, where both Armies stood looking on each other, while our Bridges were laying, which took us till near Sun-set, at which Time the Duke finding *Villars* did not offer to stir from his Ground, he order'd the Army to pass. Gen. *Rofs* with the Right Wing of Horse, and some Grenadiers were order'd to bring up the Rear; and by the Time it was Day-Light, our Army was pass'd, the Bridges taken up, and we on a full March to *Bouchain*.

Villars not offering the least Attempt to disturb us in passing, which shews what a Terror the Duke of *Marlboro'* struck into *France*, who were but the other Day the Bullies of all *Europe*; and it also shews, that all their former Conquests were not so much owing to the Bravery of their Troops, as to the Perfidiousness of their Grand Monarch.

Bouchain being the Post which my Lord had fix'd upon, is strongly situated in this great Morass that was the Barrier of the Kingdom, at which Place the *Scheld* and *Senfet* joins; wherefore, for carrying on the Siege, he was obliged to divide his Army. He therefore the next Morning after he came before it, order'd Bridges to be laid on the *Scheld* and Morass below the Town: and Gen. *Fagel*, with 30 Battalions and 40 Squadrons, to pass over, in order to carry on the Siege on that Side, which was the most commodious Part to be attack'd, and also for keeping open our Communication with *Doway*, and other Garrisons on that Side.

Villars, to prevent our taking *Bouchain*, exerted the uttermost of his Skill. The Day we came before it he march'd his Army on that Side the *Scheld*, and

G encamp'd

encamp'd with the greatest Part along the River, as near *Bouchain*, as the Morass and the Duke's Army would permit him; the other Part he pass'd over the Morass and *Senfett*, and encamp'd them on the Height of *Wavershein*, within less than a League of *Bouchain*, where they fell immediately to work in fortifying that Post with a very strong Intrenchment round the Top of that Hill, from whence they had a Communication-Line thro' the Morass along the *Senfett* to the Town, by which *Villars* proposed to prevent our carrying on the Siege on that Side. When the Duke first saw *Villars* take Post on that Hill, he thought it was with Design to fall upon *Fagel*; whereupon he order'd him to march back the same Evening he had pass'd (our Regiment was here with *Fagel*) and early next Morning Lieut. Gen. *Cadogan* with 20 Squadrons, and 16 Battalions, was order'd to join *Fagel*, and march to the other Side again. *Villars*'s Men continued hard at Work all the Night and next Day on the Hill of *Wavershein*; whereupon the Duke seeing that Post would be very troublesome to us in carrying on the Siege, order'd the next Morning all the Troops on this Side to march, and dislodge those on *Wavershein*. When we were got near the Intrenchments, several Companies of Grenadiers were order'd to march away to the Regiment to the Top of the Hill, in order to attack that Part of the Works. When we were got thither we were posted in a standing Field of Wheat, within less than 80 Paces of them, where we waited for Orders to begin the Attack. I must confess I did not like the Aspect of the Thing; besides, we thought the Duke had kept on the other Side to observe *Villars*, lest he should attack his Camp while we were attacking the Intrenchments: But while I was thus musing, up comes the Duke alone, and

of the Duke of Marlborough.

placed himself a little on the Right of my Company, from whence we had a fair View of most of their Works. Certainly, nothing ever gave me more Pleasure than the Sight of the Duke at this Juncture: he staid about five or six Minutes, and return'd; during which Time, I was in much more Pain for him than myself: for we plainly saw their Cannon pointed upon him, and the Intrenchment as full of Men as it would hold, and only waited their coming on.

But my Lord had not been longer gone than he stood by us, when Orders came for us to draw off, which we were not long about; and before the Enemy perceiv'd us going off, we were got so far down the Hill, that we were under their Fire before they let fly at us, so that we got off without the Loss of a Man, tho' they pour'd Vollies of great and small Shot after us. All the rest of the Troops drew off at the same Time, after whom they also fired their Cannon with great Fury, and kill'd several Men. The Duke ordered the Troops to march faster than ordinary, to get out of Reach, which *Villars* perceiving, drew out all the Horse he had there, and pressed hard upon our Rear; this made us still make the more Haste till we had got on the other side a rising Ground that was before us; when we passed the Right of it, the Duke seeing *Villars* still pressing on, ordered all his Squadrons to face about; and as soon as *Villars* appear'd on the Top of the Hill, they charg'd him with such Resolution, that they broke through those that first appeared, and had certainly either kill'd or taken *Villars*, had not a Brigadier, who seeing his General in this Danger, come up with fresh Squadrons to his Relief, which sav'd the Marshal, but the Brigadier and his Squadrons paid dear for it; for he was desperately wounded and taken Prisoner, and most of his

1711. Men cut to pieces, and *Villars* with the reft of his fhattered Squadrons fcour'd back as faft as they could. This Brigadier, when *Vendome* commanded, had taken *Cadogan* Prifoner on a Foraging Command, and had treated him with great Civility ; and now *Cadogan* having it in his Power, made a fuitable Return; he fent him in his Coach to his own Quarters, and there had all the Care that was poffible taken of him, till he was thoroughly recovered and cured of his Wounds, and then fent back.

As foon as this Flourifh of *Villars* was over, the Duke call'd all the Inginiers together to know whether they could carry on the Siege without removing the Enemy from *Waverfhein*; to which all anfwered in the Negative, except Col. *Armftrong*, who faid that it was to be done, and that he would undertake the moft difficult Part. The Duke knowing the Capacity of the Man, was very well pleas'd, and bid him proceed ; for he was refolv'd to have *Bouchain*, coft what it would; all that he had done would have fignified nothing without it.

Upon which ten Battalions, and as many Squadrons were ordered to march as foon as it was dark, into the Valley that was between the rifing Ground on our Side and *Waverfhein*, where we ftood to our Arms all Night, while Col. *Armftrong* with 5000 Workmen were throwing up Works on the rifing Ground behind us. When Day began to appear, we were ordered to draw out of the Valley; the Horfe march'd ftraight to their Ground, and the Foot into the Works that were thrown up, where we were furprized to find a noble large Redoubt with a double Fauffee before it, the Standard of our *Britifh* Train flying, and a Battery of 24 Cannon mounted, with which the Colonel faluted the Enemy at *Waverfhein*; he had alfo carried on an Intrenchment from this Redoubt

doubt down to the Morass, which was a prodigious 1711.
Work for in one Night.

Our ten Battalions were reliev'd in the Evening, at which Time we pitch'd our Tents, which was the first Time our Regiment had done so since we march'd from *Villarbrulin*, this being the 25th of *July*. Colonel *Armstrong* having finish'd his Work, proceeded with a Line of Circumvallation, from the Redoubt round our Camp to the Bridges below the Town, and so round the Duke's Camp, till he brought it to the *Scheld* above the Town; after which, with great Labour and Fatigue, and a vast Number of Fascines, he carried this prodigious Work through the Morass, tho' the Enemy by shutting up the Sluice of *Bouchain* had rais'd an Innundation therein; and, having laid Bridges both over the *Scheld* and *Senset*, he attack'd and drove the Enemy out of the Communication Line, and so clos'd his Circumvallation, by which all Relief was cut off from *Bouchain*. This was a most surprizing Undertaking of the Colonel's, who by constant Application finish'd it in less Time than could be imagined, by which he deservedly gain'd great Applause. And now the Communication between *Waversbein* and the Town being cut off, we open'd our Trenches, and in less than three Weeks the Governor was obliged to surrender, the Garrison being made Prisoners of War, notwithstanding our Trenches were cannonaded, as well from *Waversbein*, as the Town.

Thus ended the Duke of *Marlbro*'s last Campaign, which may truly be reckon'd amongst the greatest he ever made.

And now, after this great Man had reduced the Common Enemy of *Europe* to the last Extremity, had taken the last Barrier of his Kingdom, which lay now open to the Allies, his Army dispirited, and

1711. their Courage, and his whole Nation in a moſt miſerable Condition; I ſay, after he had done all theſe great Things ſo much to the Honour of the *Britiſh* Nation, was he ignominiouſly traduc'd, and turn'd out of all Employ, and even forc'd to fly his Country, of which he had been ſo great an Ornament; and this done by a Set of vile profligate Men, who had inſinuated themſelves into the Favour of the weak Queen, and were at this Time carrying on a ſcandalous underhand Treaty with the Grand Enemy of *Europe*. But I am here wandering out of my Way, ſo ſhall leave that ungrateful Subject, and proceed to the laſt Campaign of this War.

1712. In the Beginning of *May*, the Duke of *Ormond*, a good-natur'd, but a weak and ambitious Man, fit to be made Tool of by a Set of crafty Knaves, came over Captain General in the Room of the Duke of *Marlbro'*, and aſſembled the Army near *Doway*, where Prince *Eugene* came with a much greater Number of *Germans* than he had had at any time before, ſo that our Army conſiſted of 295 Squadrons, and 145 Battalions, which amounted to 122,000 fighting Men. Prince *Eugene* at his firſt coming had ſome Intimation from *England* that the Duke was not to act againſt *France*, on account of a ſeparate Peace between *England* and *France*, which was near a Cloſe; upon which the Prince went to the Duke, and deſir'd to know if he had ſuch Orders, that he might take his Meaſures accordingly. The Duke aſſured him, that his Orders were as full as ever the Duke of *Marlbro*'s were; and that he was ready to march againſt the Enemy when he pleaſed. The Prince was highly pleaſed at this; ſo three Days after, being the 1ſt of *May*, our whole Army march'd, and paſſing the *Scheld* a little below *Bouchain*, we advanc'd and encamp'd at *Selemvery*, near the Borders of *Piccardy*.

of the Duke of Marlborough. 103

cardy. Villars was at this Time encamp'd with his Left at *Cambray*, and his Right extending along the *Scheld* towards the upper End of that River, whofe Army did not exceed 100,000. —— Upon our coming to this Ground, the Duke and Prince agreed to ride out next Morning to take a View of *Villars's* Situation. Accordingly Orders were given for all the Grenadiers in the Army, and 100 Squadrons to march by Break of Day, in order to cover our Generals; and according to thefe Orders we march'd. Our *Britifh* Grenadiers being on the Left, advanced into *Piccardy*, where we found nothing but empty Houfes, the Peafants being all fled with their Effects; but upon our returning to Camp in the Evening, we found the Face of Affairs quite chang'd from the glorious Expectation of marching towards *Paris*, to that of a full Stop put to our Carreer; for our Managers at Home being apprehenfive that the Duke's Ambition might prompt him to do fomething that might overturn all their Meafures; therefore they fent Sir *Thomas Hanmer* Exprefs to the Duke, with Orders for him not to act againft *France*, until he received further Inftructions. Sir *Thomas* thought to have overtaken him at *Doway*; but when he came to *Tournay*, he had an Account that the Army decamp'd that Morning, and were in a full March towards *France* : This made Sir *Thomas* fpeed away from thence; fo that it was One in the Morning before he arriv'd at the Duke's Quarters. —— The Duke fent the Prince an Account of his Orders, and defired to be excus'd, in that he could not ride out with him according to Promife. Thus ended the Glory of the *Britifh* Arms after a moft inglorious Manner.

It has been much difputed, Whether the Duke of *Ormond*, upon fo extraordinary an Occafion, might not have

1712.

have refus'd obeying those Orders Sir *Thomas* brought, considering they were not sign'd by the Queen, but only by *Bolingbroke*? However, be that as it will, had the Duke done as his brave Father the Earl of *Ossory* did at the Battle of *St. Dennis*, near *Mons*, who at that Time commanded the *British* Troops under the Prince of *Orange*, and having received positive Orders from King *Charles* II. not to engage in any Action against *France* while the Treaty of *Nimeguen* was carrying on, which Orders he shew'd the Prince: After some Time the Prince sent for him, and told him he designed next Morning to attack the Enemy, and desir'd to know what he would do upon that Occasion. To which the Earl answer'd, Your Highness knows my Orders; yet when-ever I see you engag'd, I will not look on, but will rather lose my Head than the Honour of my Country; and accordingly, next Day, he, at the Head of the *British* Troops, did Wonders. And what was the Consequence? why truly the King would not venture to call him publickly to an Account, lest he should incense the Nation, who glories in nothing more than the Behaviour of their gallant Troops; and tho' he got a private Reprimand from the King, yet he had the Thanks and Approbation of the whole Nation; and had the Son follow'd the Example of his brave Father, pray who durst have call'd him to an Account, when it was evident the Consequence must have turn'd to the greatest Advantage, both to the Nation and common Cause of *Europe*? But alas! this weak Man was strangely impos'd upon by the Lord *Bolingbroke*, who not only made him his Tool, but had also impos'd both on the Queen, and the whole Nation, by his base underhand Dealing with *France*, and his bringing about that scandalous Treaty of *Utrecht*.

Notwithstanding this Disappointment, Prince *Eugene* rode out, and reconnoiter'd *Villars*, who at first Sight of our Troops thought our whole Army was on their March to *France*, which strangely alarm'd him, and thought the Duke of *Ormond* thro' Ambition of Glory had been prevail'd on by Prince *Eugene* to break thro' what he had been assur'd was privately concerted between both Courts; whereupon in a great Hurry he order'd his Train and heavy Baggage to make the best of their Way to the other Side the *Soam*, and was getting ready to decamp; but he soon found out the true Meaning, and was also inform'd by a Courier from the Duke of the Orders he had receiv'd, which put *Villars* into a better Humour. Prince *Eugene* finding how Matters went, resolv'd to make the best of his Time. While the Duke continu'd in those Parts, he therefore propos'd the taking of *Quesnoy* and *Landrescis*, and drawing a Line from the latter to *Bouchain*, the which would cover his Garrisons, and also block up *Valenshein* and *Conde*; whereupon he desir'd the Duke would cover him, while he was carrying on those Sieges, which the Duke promis'd to do, so long as he continu'd here, but at the same time told him that he expected Orders every Day for his marching off, and then he must take Care of himself; upon which the Prince march'd to *Quesnoy* with the *German* and *Dutch* Forces; at which time he posted the Earl of *Albemarle* with a Body of 14,000 Men at *Denain*, two Leagues below *Bouchain*, on the *Scheld*, to keep open a Communication with the Garrisons on the other Side, from whence he was to have all his Stores, &c. *Albemarle* fell immediately to work in fortifying his Post, and the Duke lent him as many of his Pontoons as laid two Bridges over the River, Prince *Eugene* having Occasion to make use of his own at

the

the Sieges; so that he left more than laid one Bridge. The same Day the Prince march'd to *Quesnoy*, the Duke with his *British* and Auxiliaries cross'd the *Sele*, and encamp'd at *Chateau-Cambressis*, which lyes just on the Borders of *Picardy*; here we lay with the *Sele* in our Front till *Quesnoy* was taken. Prince *Eugene* having taken that Place, march'd to *Landresseis*, which was the greatest Oversight that General ever made, considering, that at this Juncture the *French* had deliver'd *Dunkirk* into the Hands of the *English*; that *Villars* was greatly reinforced from the *Rhine*, and all the Garrisons about him; and that the Duke of *Ormond* had receiv'd his Orders for marching off with his Troops.

Next Day, after the Prince sate down before *Landressis*, the 16th of *July*, O. S. the Duke march'd off with his *British* Troops; but all the Auxiliaries, except two *Holstein* Regiments, one of Foot, and one of Dragoons, refused marching with him; the rest march'd, and join'd Prince *Eugene*. Our first Day's March was to *Uvointeseck*, near *Bouchain*, where a Cessation of Arms between *England* and *France* was declared at the Head of every Regiment; for which the Duke expected great Huzza's, but instead of that, nothing was heard but a general Hiss and Murmur through the whole Camp, which gave the Duke and his Creatures great Offence, and they term'd it the height of Ingratitude, for bringing them from having their Brains knock'd out. *Villars*, the same Day, declared the like Cessation of Arms in his Camp, and sent Officers of Distinction to compliment the Duke upon it. This Evening the Duke sent to *Denain* for the Pontoons he lent the Earl of *Albemarle*; nor could all that either the Earl, Prince *Eugene*, or the Field Deputies say, prevail with him to leave them but for eight Days, and they would lie
under

of the Duke of Marlborough. 107

under any Obligation to return them to any Place the 1712.
Duke should name; but he would upon no Account
leave them behind him, so had them taken up, and
they met us on the March. Next Day we had a
Report, how true I can't say, that two *French* Engineers in Disguise went with those that went to take
up the Pontoons; who made such Observations on
Albemarle's Works, as served their Purpose. However, I cannot believe the Duke knew any thing of
it; but his Conduct in this Affair was very much
censured, and gave his Enemies a Handle to say, that
Matters had been concerted between him and those
sent by *Villars*.

Our second Day's March was to *Auchrin*.

Next Morning very early, as we were preparing
to march, we heard great fireing towards *Denain*;
on which we concluded that *Villars* was attacking that
Post; which was confirm'd the Day following, by a
fulsome Letter from the Marshal to the Duke; wherein, after giving an Account of the Action, and the
Success attending it, he then extols the Duke to the
Skies, for his consummate Conduct and Courage, his
Loyalty to his Royal Mistress's Commands; and
concludes, that the Courage of the Allies was gone
off with the brave *British* Troops.

This Letter the Duke took Care to have made
known to the Army, several Copies of it being hand-
ed about, which indeed ought rather to be burnt;
for it made those that wish'd well to the Allies believe, that he had not acted fairly by them. 'Tis
most certain, that the Want of the Pontoons was the
Loss of *Denain*; for Prince *Eugene* having some
Notice of *Villars*'s Design, march'd the Evening before the Action, with the greatest Part of his Army,
from *Landresseis*, and was up Time enough to have
suc-

1712. succour'd *Albemarle*; but by the Time he got to the *Scheld*, the Bridge was broke by the Crowd of Baggage they had been sending over; so that he was not able to give *Albemarle* the least Assistance, but look'd on, and saw his Fate. From *Auchin*, we continued by easy Marches to *Ghent*;

Which put an End to this War, and our scandalous Part of the Campaign.

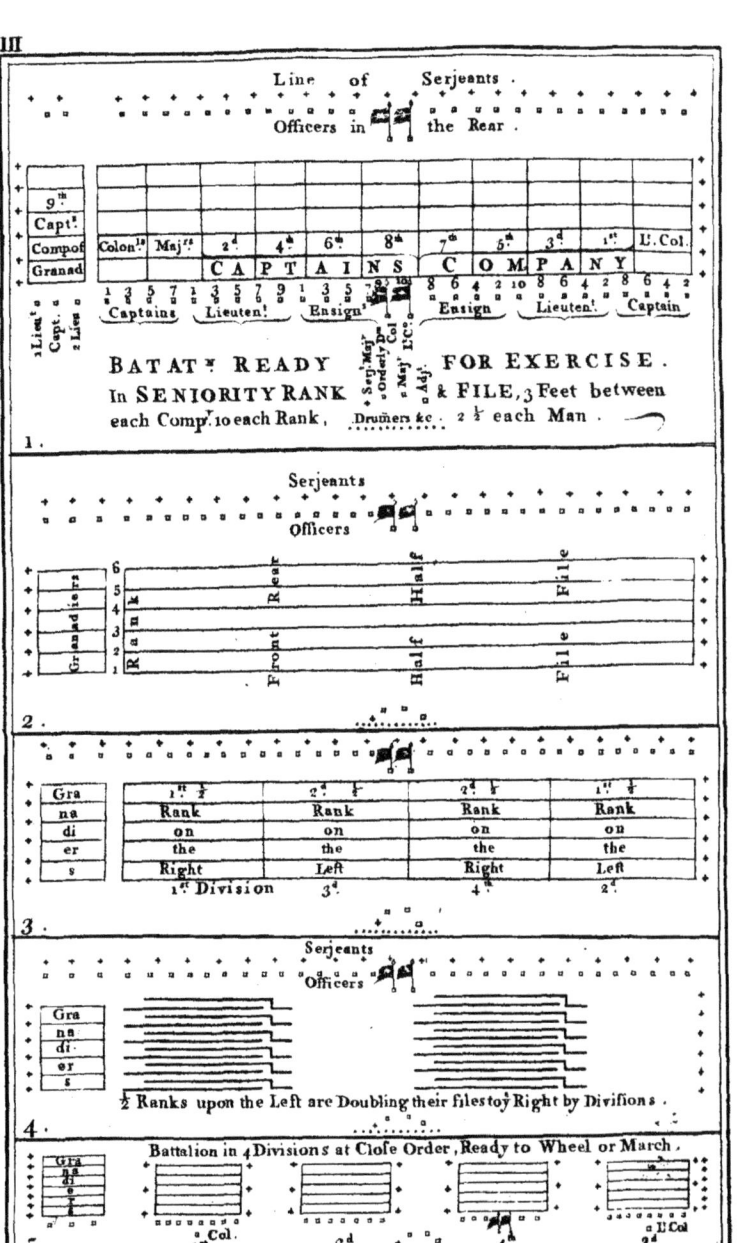

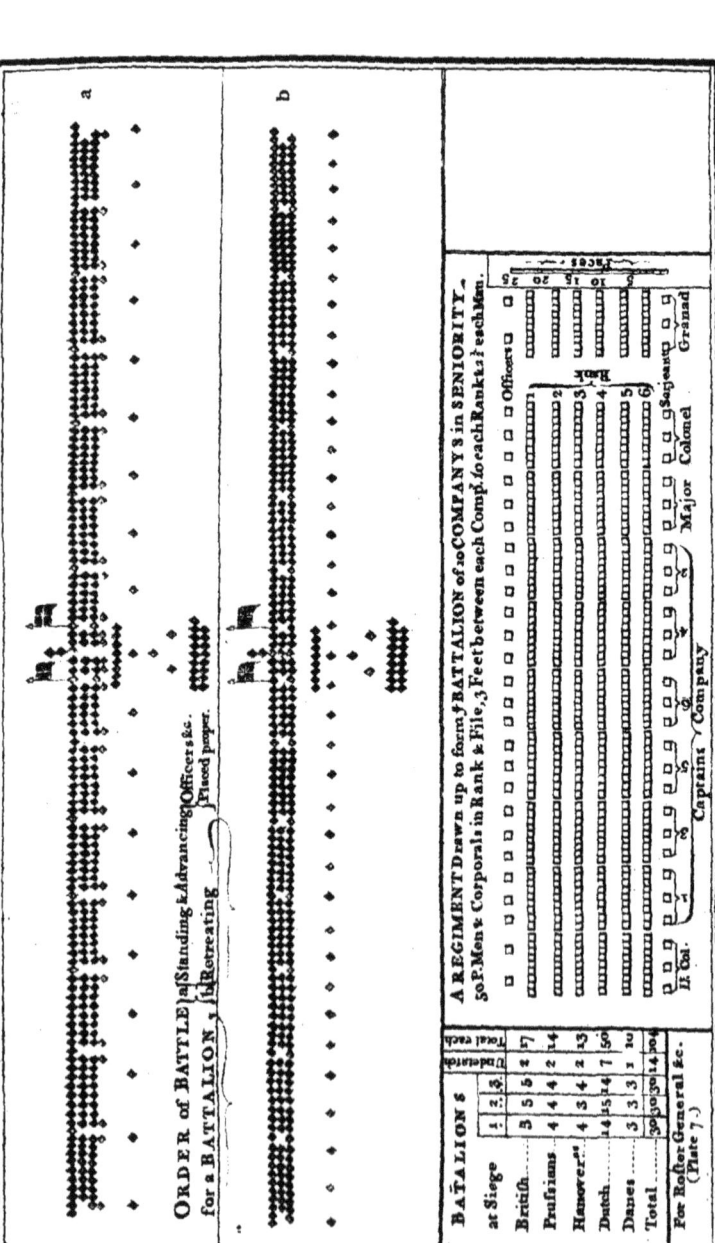

XII SQUADRONS DRAWN-UP 3 Deep *at* CLOSE-ORDER;

12 Feet *From the* Fore Feet *of the* Front Rank, *to the* Fore Feet *of the* 2d & *so on to the* Rear.

12 SQUADRONS MOUNTED N.o *of* Men & Files *in each*.		Length *of each* Rank *from* Right *to* Left 2 Feet 7 Inch.s *ea.* Man		OUTSIDE CIRCLES *of y.e* RANKS in Wheeling *a* Squadron exceeds *viz.t the*			
				SECOND y.e FRONT.		THIRD y.e SECOND.	
Men	Files	Feet	Inches	Feet	Inches	Feet	Inches
48	16	41	4	1	8 ½	4	9 ½
60	20	51	8	1	4 ½	3	11
72	24	62	.	1	1 ¾	3	4
84	28	72	4	-	11 ¾	2	10 ¾
96	32	82	8	-	10 ¼	2	6 ⅔
108	36	93	-	-	9 ¼	2	3 ¼
120	40	103	4	-	8 ¼	2	¾
132	44	113	8	-	7 ½	1	10 ½
144	48	124	-	-	7	1	8 ⅔
156	52	134	4	-	6 ½	1	7
168	56	144	8	-	6	1	5 ¾
180	60	155	-	-	5 ½	1	4 ½

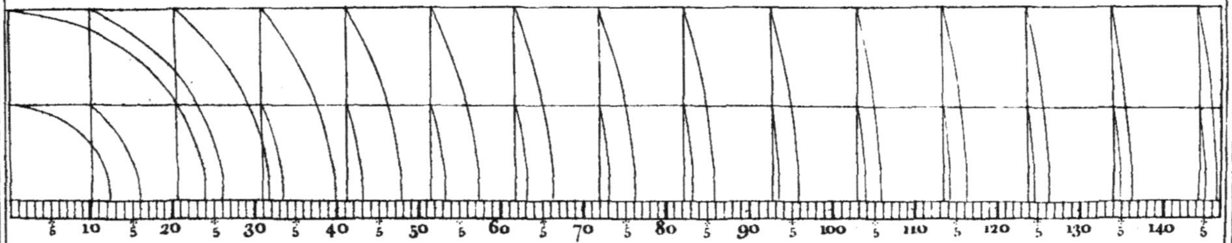

XIV.

CARTEL to EXCHANGE PRISONERS of WAR
In 14 Days Officers &c of = Rank 1 for 1 or Pay for

Officer	Livres		Officer	Livres
Mareschal or Comander	50000		Wagon Master Genl.	150
Capt. Genl.	40000		His Lieut.	80
Gen. & Lt. Genl.	20000		Comissary Genl. Transports	150
Great Mr. Ordnance			Lieut.	50
Mareschal de Camp	4000		Conductors	10
Colonel Horse			Judge	25
General Dragoons			Capt. Guides	80
Mr. de Camp Horse	3500		Lieut.	50
General Dragoons			Cornet	35
Comissary Genl. Horse	3000		Horse Guides as Troopers	20
Intendt. Armies or Provinc	5000		Chief Ingineers	500
Comissioners under them	1500		*Months Pay for others*	
Lt. Genls. Ordnance	1000		**ORDNANCE**	
	1500		Col. or Particr. Lieut.	400
Maj. Genls. Horse or Foot	800		Provinc. Comissary	250
Brigadrs.	600		or Lieut. Col.	
Major Brigad	300		Comissary Ord. or Major	150
Qr. Mr. Gl.	500		Extraordy.	30
s Adjutt.	100		Captns.	50
Adj. Gl. King or Dauphin	500		Gunners &c.	7½
to y Gl. in Chief LtGl. &Mr. deCam	300		**GENS D'ARMS**	
Qr. Mr. Genl. Horse			Brigadr.	1100
Adjutants	100		Capt. Captl. Lt. &cl. 1st & 2d Lieut.	2000
Treasr. Genl. Extra Exp. War	1500		Undr. (Scots Eng Queen Dauph)	
First Comissary	500		Lieut. Burgundy Anjou Bery	
other Army &c	50		& Orleans	
Genl. Provost	300		Major	1000
Kings Attorney	250		(Kings Guards du Cor	
Provost Lieut	100		Ensns. Guidon Gl. Arms	
Clerks	80		(Scots Troop & Cornet	
other Officers Council War	18		Lt. D'Orleans Guard Ens. Gend Arm	

4 to 15 Soldiers *under a* Brigade & Exempt | Cornet Light Horse Guidon Scots 600
Lieut. or Provost *with* Horses Arms &c niqr | Eng. & Gl. Arms Majr. Gr. du Cor
ESCORT *y* Attorney, Fiscal, Assessor & Clerks | Exempts Qr. Mast. Brig. Sub Dr.
unmolested to Seize, Try &c. Thieves keep 2 | said Troops &c. Granadr. for Horse Month Pay
Leagues from either Army &c Over or Under said | Kr. or Queens Guards
Numbr. *lawfull* Prisoners.

	Guards	Horse	Dragoons	Foot & Ordnance
	Livres L s d	Livres L s d	Livres L s d	Livres L s d
Colonel	3000	400	350	400
Lieut. Col.	1500	250	250	250
Major	600	220	200	150
Captain	300	200	150	100
Subalterns &c				
Lieut.	one Months Pay	100	70	
Adjutant			60	40
Cornet undr. Lt. or Ensn.		75	55	35
Qr. Mastr. Regt.			50	25
		25	25	
Brigdrs. or Corpls.		22½	20	
Clerks Private Men		20	18	7½
Provost Lt. Clerks &c		4 0	4 0	4 0
		2 0		2 0

Col. Genl. Swiss Guards	40000	Govr. Comr. Kgs Lt. Majr. Adjut. Captns.
Serjt. Foot	15	Gates 1 Months Pay High: Posts Volunt. Courts.
Capt. Genls. Guard 1 Months Pay		of no Milit. Post 2000 Almoners Ministr.
Trumpeters return in 3 Days or pd. by y Detainr.		Physitians &c Directors Genl. & Particr. &c.
GENT. CADETS.		Hospl. Women Childn. 12 or undr. Post Boys
Capt. 9 Companys	150	Messengers Servts. with Ransom
Lieutenants	80	None to be Stripd or Prefs'd to Serve
Sub. Do. or Ensigns	60	Private Men to have 3 fr Serjt. no. 6 & Bread
Serjeants	20	Offr. treated as they can afford, if on Parole to
Corporals	12	surendr. 14 Days after Ratificatn. of y Treaty
Cadets	10	if not clear'd, Acct. every 6 Months. Lead Bullets

Trumpr. Drumr. no Ransom unless they had } onlyus'd none Ram'd For Flying Parties
Arms in hand when taken, then pay as Troop or Sold. Prison. give notice where confin'd. (Skirmishes)
Parties undr. 15 Horseor y Punish. unless Broke by

DISCIPLINE
FOR A
Regiment of FOOT upon ACTION.
ALSO,
The most ESSENTIAL DISCIPLINE
OF THE
CAVALRY.

GREAT Pains have been taken to bring our Troops under one Method of Discipline, but most Officers persisting on having some trifling Motions perform'd after their own Whims, more than the essential Parts of Discipline; *i. e.* how they are to act when they come to face the Enemy. Our last formal piece of Discipline was entitled, *An Exercise for the Horse, Dragoons, and Foot, By Authority*; which Words oblige the whole Army to conform.

It is surprizing, after two such Wars as our Nation have been engaged in, that so poor a Performance should be skreen'd by Authority. And it is strange, that we have nothing relating to Action introduced into our Discipline. How preposterous is it to see some of our *English* Jack-Boot-Men, with all their Accoutrements, perform an Exercise on Foot! Was this ever known to be of Use upon Action? Is it possible for young Gentlemen that never saw any thing

thing of Action, (of whom the Army in a short Time will be composed) to form an Idea of Action, out of this Book of Discipline?

Every one will allow, that 'tis absolutely necessary that the Troops should be brought under one Method of Discipline; that when His Majesty shall please to order them together, or a General Officer is to receive them, they may perform a graceful Exercise. And were there 20 Battalions on one Field, they might answer each other in their Firings with all the Regularity imaginable; but then they are not to keep popping by single Platoons.

Discipline of HORSE.

It is sufficient for them to ride well, to have their Horses well managed, and train'd up to stand Fire; that they take particular Notice what Part of the Squadron they are in, their Right and Left-Hand Men, and File-Leaders, that they may, when they happen to break, readily know to form. Breaking their Squadrons ought to be practised in their common Discipline. That they MARCH and WHEEL with a Grace, and HANDLE their SWORDS well; which is the only Weapon our *British* Horse makes use of when they charge the Enemy; more than this is superfluous. The Duke of *Marlborough* would allow the Horse but three Charges of Powder and Ball to each Man for a Campaign, and that only for guarding their Horses when at Grass, and not to be made use of on Action.

DRAGOONS

Should be well instructed in the Use of Arms, having often Occasion to make use of them on Foot; but when on Horseback, they are to fight as the Horse do. I shall

page 111

A BATALION making its 4 several FIRINGS

A

Colonel ⊙

Drum. ⊙

B

Col.ˡ ⊙

Dʳ. ⊙

C

D

Col.ˡ ⊙

Dʳ. ⊙

$\left.\begin{array}{l}A.\\B.\\C.\\D.\end{array}\right\}$ the $\left\{\begin{array}{l}1\\2\\3\\4^{th}\end{array}\right\}$ Fire or Reserve

Regiment of FOOT upon ACTION.

I shall be as brief as the Nature of the Subject will admit; nor shall I take Notice of the Manual Exercise, or Evolutions, but refer to the Book of Exercise. I must say, there is no Occasion for puzzling the Soldiers with more Evolutions than is necessary to form the Battalion for Action.

There is not yet any Method found to train up our Infantry for Action in the Field, otherwise than by representing one Battalion engaging another; I shall therefore lay down the best Method I can for that Purpose. In order to which, I must first suppose our Battalion to consist of 800, or 1000 Men. Let us suppose our Battalion drawn up with the Army on the Field of Battle, three deep, their Bayonets fix'd on their Muzzles, the Grenadiers divided on the Flanks, the Officers ranged in the Front; and the Colonel, or, in his Absence, the Lieutenant-Colonel (who, I suppose, fights the Battalion) on Foot, with his Sword drawn in his Hand, about eight or ten Paces in the Front, opposite the Centre, with an expert Drum by him. He should appear with a chearful Countenance, never in a Hurry, or by any Means ruffled; and to deliver his Orders with great Calmness, and Presence of Mind.

The first Thing the Colonel should do, is to order the Major and Adjutant to divide the Battalion into four grand Divisions, which is to be the Groundwork of all our Performances, of which our *Martinet* gives but a faint Idea. I find he knows very little of the Consequences attending our Grand Divisions; for from them we form our Platoons, our Sub-Divisions in all our Marchings; and from them we form the Hollow Square, as well standing as marching; and that after a much more commodious and readier Way, than the round-about Way now practised; for each of our Grand Divisions make a Front of the Square, so that in marching out there, there is no further Occasion for square-marking out the Ground; and the Officers of the Platoons may at once know what Fireing they'll be off in the Square, as well as in the Battalion; which will save Time and Trouble. When Pikes were in Use, our Battalions were composed but of three Grand Divisions, *viz.* one of Pikes in the Centre, and a Division of Musketeers on the Right and Left of them; but since Pikes have been laid aside, a Battalion cannot be disposed for Action, but by dividing it into four Grand Divisions. Our Battalions thus divided, and each Division distinguished by the

$$\left.\begin{array}{l} 1. \text{ the Right} \\ 2. \\ 3. \text{ the Left} \\ 4. \end{array}\right\} \text{Division,}$$

Each Division to be divided in four Platoons, which, with the Grenadiers will make up eighteen; but when our Infantry is on the low Establishment, as in time of Peace, our Grand Divisions will admit but of three Platoons to each, and those but small.

The Eighteen Platoons are to be divided into three Fireings, so that there will be six in each. And as it is absolutely necessary to have a Fire in Reserve, the Front Rank is to be reserved for that Purpose, which on Occasion will make a fourth Fireing; so that the two Rear Ranks are only to go on with the Fireings, until the Commanding Officer thinks fit to order the Front Rank to fire, either by themselves, or to go on with the Rear Ranks of their Platoons; all which depends wholly on the Discretion of the Officer that fights the Battalion.

As the Commanding Officer will be exposed to the Fire of his own Men, as well as that of the Enemy,

Regiment of FOOT upon ACTION.

he is to take special Care that he keep opposite the two Centre Platoons while the other Parts of the Battalion keep Firing; and he must also take as great Care, that when it comes to the Turn of the Centre Platoons to fire, that both he and the Drum step aside, and return as soon as they have done, otherwise they must fall by their own Fire.

Note, that the Front Rank of the two Centre Platoons are to fire with their own Platoons, and not to be of the Reserve, or fourth Fire, otherwise the Commanding Officer would have no Shelter from the Fire of the Front Rank.

Upon dividing the grand Divisions into Platoons, place a Serjeant in the Interval of each Platoon, after which the Major appoints the Officers, and tells them what firing they are of, and how they are to behave; he then acquaints the Lieutenant-Colonel, and remaining Part of the Officers, that they are to march to the Rear when the others take their Platoons.

Note that, always upon Action, the Officers of the Platoons are to be posted as near their own Companies as they can, without Regard to Seniority; this being done, the Colonel takes the Management of the Battalion upon himself.

When he finds there is no avoiding coming to Battle, he is to order the Soldiers to lay down their Knapsacks, Tent-poles, and what is cumbersome, and the Serjeant sends them to some Place out of the Way, where a Serjeant with a few Men takes Care of them. If we win the Day, they will be safe; if not, 'tis no Matter what becomes of them.

When this is done, he, either by Word of Command, or the Signal of Drum, orders the Officers to take their Platoons; and when the Word *March*, or Signal of Drum is given, they march into the Intervals, and the Lieutenant-Colonel, and other Officers, march at the same time to the Rear. The Lieutenant-Colonel, or, in his Absence, the eldest Captain, posts himself eight or ten Paces from the Rear Rank opposite the Center, the rest of the Officers posting themselves four Paces from the Rear Rank, extending to the Right and Left to cover the Battalion, where they will be of as great Use as those in the Front, in seeing that the Soldiers keep up in their Ranks and do their Duty. The Ensigns that carry the Colours ought to be able-body'd Men, who are to post themselves in the Centre Rank, on the Right and Left of the two Centre Platoons, as they are mark'd in the Plan of the first Firing, which shews the whole; they are to carry the Colours always well advanced. When Musters fall into their Platoons, the Serjeants that were plac'd there fall into the Intervals of the Rear Rank, where they are to be assisting the Officers in seeing the Platoons do their Duty; the remaining Part of the Serjeants are to post themselves on the Flanks and in the Rear between the Officers and Soldiers, where they will be also of great Use in seeing the Soldiers do their Duty. The Drums are to be divided into three Parts, on the Right and Left, and behind the two Centre Platoons, all to range in a Line with the Serjeants, but not to Beat without Orders. The Major and Adjutant having seen all these Matters settled, post themselves on the Flanks, from whence they are to observe, as much as in them lies, the Behaviour of the Battalion, but to take great Care that they ride not into the Front while the Battalion is firing.

Our Battalion being thus form'd for Battle, and as it were riveted together, so that no Soldier can possibly misbehave, but there will be an Eye presently upon him; and nothing but the Want of Care and Resolution in the Officers can make a Battalion thus form'd

Regiment of FOOT upon ACTION.

form'd mifcarry, unlefs over-power'd by Numbers, or fome unforefeen Accident.

Before we enter upon Action, I muft firft take Notice of one Thing, hitherto overlook'd by all; that is, the Ufe of the DRUM on many more Occafions than is generally made of it. For Inftance, it is not every Commanding Officer that has a Voice capable to go through the Management of a Battalion when in common Exercife, much more in the Hurry of Action. Would it not be a Shame for him to order the Major or Adjutant, in the Day of Battle, to fight the Battalion, and he only a Cypher at the Head of it, and pretend he has not a Voice to go thro' it?

I am forry to fay there has always been too many indolent Sparks in the Army, who would think it very hard fhould a diligent experienc'd Officer be put over their Heads.

I was once at a Review, when the Commanding General of the Troops was reviewing a Regiment of Foot, where were prefent the Colonel, Lieutenant-Colonel, Major, and moft of all the Captains, and yet not one of them capable of going thro' the Difcipline of the Regiment, of which the General very juftly took publick Notice.

This is only a Hint, to caution our young Gentlemen, even from the Colonels themfelves to the Enfigns, that none of them may think themfelves above learning their Duty. I am for introducing the more frequent Ufe of the Drum, as well upon Action, as in the common Exercife of a Regiment, to affift the Voice.

Suppofe the Commanding Officer fhould happen to be killed, the Voice of him that fupplies his Place may be fo different ftom the other's, that it may occafion a Confufion; whereas the Drum is always the fame, and much eafier heard and underftood, efpecially

cially when the Men are train'd up by, and constantly us'd to it. A great deal more might be said in Favour of this warlike Instrument; however I would not be so understood, as that the Drum is wholly to be depended on. No, I am only for introducing the more frequent Use of it purely to assist the Voice; for the Commanding Officer must, on all Occasions, first apprize both Officers and Soldiers what they are about to do, and when he has done that, proceed as he shall think fit, either by the Word of Command, or by the Drum; so that, I say, 'tis absolutely necessary for the Soldiers to be train'd up by both, since 'tis impossible that any Inconveniency can accrue thereby, and that it is most certain it may, on many Occasions, be of great Use; wherefore I see no Reason why our Infantry should not be train'd up by the Drum, as well in their Firings, or rather more, than the Manual Exercise; so that, as it often happens in the Hurry of Action, when it is not possible for the Voice to be heard, that then the Drum will be of the greatest Consequence.

Use of the DRUM *in Action.*

Suppose that the Signal for Battle is given: Upon this the Colonel orders his Drum to beat a Ruffle, which is as much as to say, *Take Care*; and then saying something to encourage and excite the Men to the Performance of their Duty. This may seem ridiculous by some, yet I know 'twill animate and raise an Emulation among the Soldiers, especially when they have a LOVE for their OFFICERS. I cannot but take Notice of some Gentlemen, who instead of treating their Men with GOOD NATURE, use them with CONTEMPT and CRUELTY; by which those Gentlemen often meet with their FATE in the Day of Battle,

tle, from their own Men; when those Officers who, on the other hand, treat their Men with JUSTICE and HUMANITY, will be sure, on all Occasions, to have them stand fast by them, and even interpose between them and Death.

The Colonel having thus spoke cheerfully to the Men, he then gives the Word, MARCH; at which time the Drum beats to the March: and when the Battalion has got within four or five Paces of him, he turns to the Enemy, and marches slowly down (we will suppose to his opposite Battalion) till he finds they begin to fire upon him; upon which he orders his Drum to cease beating, and turning to the Battalion, gives the Word, HALT; and then orders his Drum to beat a Preparative, upon which the six Platoons of the first Firing make ready, as in Figure A, as does also all the Front-Rank, except those of the two Centre-Platoons, on which the two Rear-Ranks close forward, keeping their Thumbs on the Cocks, and their Arms well recover'd; and the Front-Rank kneels, placing their Butts on the Ground by their Left-Feet, where all are to wait for the next Word of Command, or Signal of the Drum, from the Colonel himself; for we are not now to fire by single Platoons, as is generally pract's'd at Reviews, which will not do when we come to engage the Enemy; nor will they carry such Weight with them, or do near the Execution that six Platoons will do, when pour'd in all together upon them: wherefore, 'tis the Colonel himself must give Orders for firing the Platoons, and not the Officers belonging to them, who are only to see that the Soldiers do their Duty, and observe such Orders as the Colonel shall give, whether by his Voice, or the Drum. And let no one say, what Occasion is there for Officers to the Platoons, when they are not to give the Word of Command? But let them confider, that both Officers and Serjeants will have enough to do to take Care that their Platoons perform their Duty in every Refpect; and when they find it requifite, they are to tell them foftly what they are to do, but fo as none muft hear them but their own Men; and if they perform this well it will be fufficient, and will contribute much towards the Behaviour of the Battalion. The Commanding Officer is the beft Judge when they are, or are not to fire; for, tho' our Platoons are made ready, yet perhaps the Enemy by this time may have retreated, and got out of Reach of our Shot: whereupon, inftead of going on with our Firing, the Colonel orders them to half-cock their Fire-locks, &c. and proceeds in marching after them, rather than throw away his Fire, which would in Courfe be done, were the Officers of the Platoons to give the Word of Command for their Firing, as is done on Reviews. But let us fuppofe the Enemy ftand their Ground, or perhaps advance to meet us; upon which our fix Platoons being made ready, as above, and waiting the Colonel's Orders, who, if he finds his Voice not fufficient to go thro' his Bufinefs, he then orders his Drum to beat a Flam; at which time the Front-Rank drop their Muzzles to the Ground, and the two Rear-Ranks prefent. Now the Officers and Serjeants of thefe Platoons are to take great Care that the Soldiers level well their Arms, fo that their Fire may have Effect on the Enemy; as alfo caution them to wait the next Signal of Drum (here the Men ought in training them to be us'd to that of recovering their Arms fometimes inftead of firing, which will make them take Care in waiting for Orders to fire.)

The Platoons being prefented, the Colonel orders the Drum to beat a fecond Flam, on which they

fire,

Regiment of FOOT upon ACTION.

fire, and immediately recover their Arms, fall back, and load as faft as they can; which the Officers and Serjeants are to fee done without Hurry or Diforder. The Front-Rank remain with their Thumbs on the Cocks, and Muzzles to the Ground.

As foon as the firft Fire is made, the Colonel, without making the leaft Stop or Hefitation, orders his Drum to beat a fecond Preparative, on which the fix Platoons of the fecond Fire make ready, and go on, as in Figure B : when they have fir'd he immediately beats the third Preparative; on which the fix Platoons of the third Fire make ready, and proceed as in Figure C. And thus the Colonel continues his Firings ftanding, without Intermiffion between them; and if he fees Occafion for firing his Front-Rank, he then gives the Word, FRONT-RANK, TAKE CARE, PRESENT, FIRE, as in D.

Let us fuppofe that the Enemy be returning their Fire, and obftinately maintain their Ground : In this Cafe the Colonel is to advance upon them ; in order to which, he is firft to apprize the Battalion of it, on which the Front-Rank ftands up, keeping their Arms well recover'd : He then orders the Drum to beat a Preparative for the Platoons of the firft, or next that are to fire, to make ready ; which being done, he gives the Word MARCH ; and when the Battalion has got within two Paces of him, he turns to the Enemy, and advances in this Pofture till he comes fo near as he intends. Note, the nearer he approaches the Enemy, the nearer he is to keep to the Battalion; otherwife he would be a particular Mark to them ; and then, if he finds they ftand their Ground, he gives the Word HALT, on which the Front-Rank kneels, and the Rear-Ranks of the Platoons that are to fire, clofe forward ; he then orders the Drum to beat a Flam, on which the Front-Rank drop their Muzzles,

Muzzles, and the Rear-Ranks present; and on the next Flam they fire; and so he continues his Firings as fast as he can, until he obliges them to give Way, or perhaps, seeing us advance upon them, after the above Manner, they have already given Way. It is not possible to foresee what may happen at this critical Juncture, nor to lay down Rules how to proceed, but must leave it to the Discretion of the Commanding Officer to act as Things may offer, or according to such Orders as he may receive from the General. However,

I will suppose that the Enemy has given Ground, and put themselves on the Retreat, and are marching off as fast as they can; and consequently faster than we can propose to follow, and keep our Order, which we must not break upon any Account; so that all the Colonel can do on this Occasion, is to keep firing after them so long as his Shot will reach them, and then leave them to the Horse. Thus much for Battalions firing Standing and Advancing.

How to act, if obliged to Retreat.

This is a Matter of the greatest Consequence, and requires the greatest Conduct in a General, as well as Resolution in both Officers and Soldiers; for the least Mismanagement puts all into Confusion, especially among the Infantry, the Officers of whom will find it a very difficult Matter to keep the Soldiers from breaking, especially if they are hard press'd by the Horse; and if they are once broke, not a Man in ten escapes: however, Resolution and good Orders have surmounted great Difficulties.

In this Case, according to what I propos'd, I shall only touch upon the Retreat of our single Battalion upon this grand Occasion, *viz.* when our Colonel

Regiment of FOOT upon ACTION.

lonel finds the Army giving Way, he then orders the Battalion to face to the Right about, upon which the Drum beats the Retreat. On this Occasion the Generals are to draw as many of the Infantry together as they can, and also of the Cavalry, to assist the Infantry in getting off: But, as I am on the Retreat of our single Battalion, so I shall proceed only upon it. Our Battalion being now on the Retreat, we are to march as fast as we possibly can, so that we keep our Order, and avoid Confusion, until we are got out of Reach of our Enemies Foot, the Lieut. Colonel and Officers in the Rear leading them with their Pikes under-hand. But those Officers to the Platoons are to carry their Pikes upright in their Hands, by which they'll have much better Command of them, than either by trailing, or having them pinn'd to their Shoulders. As soon as we have got on the Retreat, the Colonel's Drum ceases beating, but still keeps by him; and the Lieut. Colonel gets a Drum by him, who is now to beat the Retreat. While the Lieut. Colonel thus leads the Battalion, the Colonel keeps a watchful Eye on the Enemy; and the Major, Adjutant, and spare Serjeants, are to take great Care that no Disorders happen on the March. If the Colonel finds the Enemy pressing upon him, he orders his Drum to beat a Preparative, on which the six Platoons or next Firing makes ready. (Note, that no one of the Front-Rank make ready but what belongs to the Platoons that are to fire.) The Platoons being made ready, they immediately face to the Left about, at which time the Front-Rank kneels, placing their Butts by their Left-Feet, and the Rear-Ranks close forward, keeping their Arms well recover'd.

The Lieut. Colonel is to take no Notice of this, or any other Preparative, but continues on his March,

unless

unless the Colonel sends him Orders to the contrary. The Officers and Serjeants, that are on the March with the Battalion, are to take great Care, that they keep open the Intervals of the Platoons that are firing, until they return; nor must the Colonel keep them too long abroad, but make them fire, if there is Occasion, as soon as possible, and then march them briskly back, keeping their Arms well recover'd till they get within their Intervals, and then load. Thus the Colonel keeps firing, and the Battalions marching, until we have got out of Reach of the Enemies Foot. We are not to lose Time, which upon this Occasion is very precious, by halting, and facing about, but to make the best Haste we can to get clear; for, if we do not out-march the Foot, pray what must be the Consequence when both Horse and Foot are up with us? Why truly, we must either stand to be cut to Pieces, or throw down our Arms, and call for Quarters, which in a manner will be much the same: for, upon all warm Pursuits there is but little Quarter to be expected. Wherefore, the first Thing we have to do is to out-march the Enemies Foot; and when once got out of their Reach, if we have but Resolution to keep our Orders, our Fire will keep off any reasonable Body of Horse, especially when any Number of Battalions get together; for too often the Horse take Care of themselves on these Occasions, and leave the Foot to do the same.

Suppose we have got clear of the Enemies Foot; but their Horse having drove our Horse out of the Field, are now marching down upon us; wherefore, to defend ourselves against them, we must think of forming the Hollow Square; but must never attempt it, while the Foot are able to come up with us.

This

Regiment of FOOT *upon* ACTION.

This was the Cafe of the *Dutch* Infantry on the Plains of *Fleury*, in 1690, where their Cavalry having mifbehaved, left the Infantry to fhift for themfelves, where Prince *Waldeck*, who commanded the *Dutch* Forces, form'd 16 Battalions into one Square, who made their Retreat over thofe Plains, till they got under the Cannon of *Charleroy*; notwithftanding all the *French* Cavalry made feveral Attempts to break in upon them, yet could not, for want of their Foot, that were not able to come up with them. Another Inftance of this Kind I was an Eye-Witnefs of, and that was, when the Duke of *Marlborough*, in 1705, pafs'd the *French* Lines in *Brabant*; where, after he had drove the Enemies Horfe out of the Field, there were ten *Bavarian* Battalions that ftuck together, and form'd themfelves into a Square, our Infantry not being able to get up with them; fo they defended themfelves againft all the Cavalry of our Right Wing, until they got under the Walls of *Lovain*; which plainly fhews, that if a Body of Foot have but Refolution to keep their Order, there is no Body of Horfe dare venture within their Fire.

If our Battalion is under a Neceffity of forming the Square by ourfelves, I prefume, any one will allow, that the moft expeditious Way, and that which tends to the leaft Confufion, to be the beft; and I believe, when every thing is confider'd, they will find the following Method to be fo, *viz.* when the Colonel finds he has no Way to fave the Battalion, but by performing the Square, which is not to be attempted but upon the laft Extremity, he fends to the Lieut. Colonel to apprize him of it, who immediately orders the Battalion to Halt; which they are to do without altering their Afpect, that no Time may be loft; on which the Colonel, without any more to do, gives the Word, TAKE CARE TO FORM THE SQUARE;

and

and then orders his Drum to beat a RUFFLE; upon which the firſt Diviſion, which is now on the Left of the Battalion, as they are fac'd, *face* to the *Right* on their RIGHT HEELS; the other three Diviſions ſtand faſt, until the Drum beats a FLAM; on which the firſt Diviſion MARCHES FORWARD, the ſecond WHEELS to the RIGHT by the RIGHT-HAND-MAN of the FRONT-RANK, as they are now fac'd; the third Diviſion MARCHES DIRECTLY FORWARD; and the fourth WHEELS *to the Left by the Left-Hand-Man of the Rear-Rank*: ſo the firſt Diviſion will take the Ground of the third, and join their three Ranks to the three Files on the Left of the fourth; and their three Files in the Rear will join the three Ranks of the Right of the ſecond. The third Diviſion marches on üntil their three Files on their Right are join'd by the three Ranks on the Right of the fourth; and their three Ranks on their Left join'd by the three Files on the Left of the ſecond, which cloſe the Square; all which, with a very little Practice, will be found very eaſy, and ready to perform. The Square being form'd, the Lieut. Colonel goes to that Face of the Square which is towards the Garriſon, or Place we are to march to, on which the Square face all that Way, and ſo proceed on their March: The Colours and ſupernumerary Officers get into the Square. The Officers to the Platoons are to march two Paces without their Intervals; as alſo the Serjeants within the Square.

The Colonel, who by this time has got on Horſeback, with the Major and Adjutant, are to keep without the Square, to have a watchful Eye on the Enemy; and to keep the Grenadiers by him, to oppoſe any ſmall Body that may be for making Attempts, or Feints, to retard our March.

Regiment of FOOT *upon* ACTION.

In our March, let us suppose that the Enemies Horse are come up with us, and are for attacking us; on this the Colonel sends to the Lieut. Colonel to Halt, he orders his Drum to beat a RUFFLE, on which they FACE SQUARE, at which time the Officers and Serjeants of the Platoons fall into their INTERVALS, and the *Colonel, Major, Adjutant,* and Grenadiers get into the SQUARE, and the *Lieut. Colonel* falls into the CENTRE-INTERVAL of that Face of the Square he leads, that he may be ready to step out, and march again the next Opportunity. On this Occasion our Square is not to fire by Platoons; nor is it possible for the Colonel, or any in the Square, to give Orders and Directions to them to fire. For suppose the Square should (as probably it may) be attack'd on all Sides, those in the Square cannot attend all Parts of it; wherefore the Colonel is to appoint the eldest Officer of each Face of the Square to fight his own Division, who are to ADVANCE two Paces before the Centre-Intervals, and are to fire by Ranks, the Rear Rank first; the Lieut. Colonel fights the Division he is in.

These four Officers have as it were four separate Commands, and are to fight their Divisions as they find themselves attack'd, without waiting for, or taking the least Notice of one another, or even so much as waiting for Orders from the Colonel. The Drum is by no means to be made use of, but all by Word of Command; and the Officers and Serjeants of the Platoons will be of great Use in seeing the Ranks do their Duty, and particularly in levelling their Arms, and waiting the Word of Command from their own Officers.

If we have Resolution to keep Order, and avoid Hurry, there is no reasonable Body of Horse dare venture upon us. It is not to be imagined, how the

Fire

Fire of one Rank will ſtop and diſorder Horſe; and then a ſecond, and a third on the Heels of it, will certainly ſend them a packing. Beſides; ſhould the Colonel ſee any one Part hard preſt, he has the Grenadiers to ruſh out, which will be no ſmall Surprize, on them: Nor has it been known, that ever a Body of Horſe alone, without the Aſſiſtance of Foot, brake in upon a Body of Foot, that with calm Reſolution made their regular Fires. So that the Havock which the Horſe generally make among the Foot, is when they find them broke.

The more Battalions that form the Square, makes it ſtill the ſtronger; and then every Commanding Officer fights his own Battalion on Foot, and fires by Platoons, as they ſhall ſee Occaſion; not by the Drum; for whenever the Square is attack'd, they muſt fire by Command.

Suppoſe we have obliged the Enemy to keep at a Diſtance; then the Colonel, Major, Adjutant, and Grenadiers, get out of the Square, and the Lieutenant-Colonel, with his Drum, to the Head of his Diviſion, and proceeds on his March; at which Time, the Colonel draws the Grenadiers to ſuch Part as may be in moſt Danger of being attack'd, and then we continue our March until we are out of all Danger.

Thus much for training up a Battalion, for their engaging another in a plain Field; as alſo in making their Retreat from Horſe: In which is ſhewn the abſolute Neceſſity of dividing our Battalions into Grand Diviſions. I am ſurprized the Army does not fall into it; which if they did, I am perſuaded they would ſoon leave off that round-about-way of forming the Square, that is now in Vogue. All that can be alledged for forming the Square after the preſent Manner, is, that they keep a Front of the fourth Part of
the

Regiment of FOOT upon ACTION.

the Battalion againſt the Enemy, to defend them whilſt forming; but ſurely this is a very weak Argument, unleſs they firſt capitulate with the Enemy, to fall upon no other Part while they are forming; if they do, they'll find them in a very unguarded Condition.

Suppoſe the Enemy to be ſo near us, when we are about forming the Square, as to make a Puſh at us while we are forming (which, by the By, ought not to be done when they are ſo near) but ſuppoſe they are, the Thing is ſo ſudden, and ſo ſoon perform'd, without facing-about, or running round the Battalion to mark out the Square, that we are form'd before they can tell what we are about; and in Caſe they ſhould make an Attempt upon us, the Colonel, inſtead of dividing the Grenadiers to the Angles, draws them together, and makes a moving Front of them, to ſupport any Part that may be in Danger of being attack'd. The Method of firing our Platoons in the Battalion, after the Manner I propoſe, is undoubtedly the only Way for engaging the Enemy; and when there are any Number of Battalions together for a Review, they may with great Regularity anſwer each other after that Manner. As to the firing in the Square, when attack'd, there is no other Way to be made uſe of, than what I have propoſed. The firing of Platoons, as now practiſed, being only adapted for making a Shew on Reviews; nor are the firing by ſingle Platoons in the Battalion, or the Street-firing, of any other Uſe. Nor can I comprehend what Uſe any of them can be upon Action. The Manner of forming the Square by Grand Diviſions, when the Battalion is faced to their proper Front, is no more than facing the three Diviſions on the Left, to the RIGHT-ABOUT, and the Diviſion on the Right to face on their Right Heels to the LEFT;

from

from whence they all march, and wheel, and join, as above, and in reducing.

The firſt Diviſion face on their Left Heels to the RIGHT, the third to the LEFT-ABOUT, the ſecond and fourth STAND FAST (that is, ſuppoſing all to be faced ſquare) and then they all march and wheel to their proper Ground.

It rarely happens that two Armies meet in a fair Plain, but one or the other takes to ſome advantageous Piece of Ground, or throws up an Intrenchment to cover them, ſo that in attacking them there frequently happens great Diſorder and Confuſion: Wherefore, in this Caſe, I ſhall take Notice of another Branch of Diſcipline, which our authorized *Martinet* knows nothing of, nor has it been practiſed many Years; a Thing ſo abſolutely neceſſary, that all Battalions ought to be conſtantly train'd to the Knowledge of it; nay, even our Horſe and Dragoons too; and that is what we call breaking the Battalion, which was much recommended by Duke *Schomberg*. I ſpoke of it to ſome good Officers, at the Time the preſent Diſcipline was firſt introduced among our Troops, but they would by no Means hearken to it, leſt it might give the Men a Habit of breaking upon every trifling Occaſion, which was the Reaſon of its being laid aſide. But as 'tis impoſſible for Battalions to climb Trenches or Ditches, without breaking, and running into great Diſorder, and often ſeveral Regiments intermingling together, as I have, upon ſome Occaſions, known it; then, ſurely, a Method ought to be put in Practice, whereby Battalions may know how they may readily form, and draw up in Order again.

NOTE, In order for reviving this uſeful Branch of Diſcipline, the following Particulars are to be ſtrictly obſerved by all the Officers and Soldiers, whenever the

Regiment of FOOT *upon* ACTION.

the Battalion is form'd, whether it be for Action, or any other Occasion (*viz.*) *The Officers are to take particular Notice which of the grand Divisions they belong to, and on which Side of the Colours they are, and who are the Officers on the Right and Left of them; on the exact Observance of this, depends the ready forming the Battalion whenever they happen to break. The Soldiers are also to take particular Notice of which Side the Colours the Division they are in lies; they must likewise take Notice who are the Officers of their Divisions, the Ranks they are in, their File-Leaders, and their Right and Left Hand Men.*

This at first may seem almost impossible to bring Men to; but when they are train'd up to it, they will find it as familiar to them as handling their Arms, and a Battalion so train'd will upon many Occasions find great Advantage.

Suppose our Battalion to be thus train'd up, and that upon some Occasion we have been oblig'd to Break, and run into great Disorder, so that Officers and Soldiers are intermingled, and all in Hurry and Confusion; this is a Consequence which frequently attends the Foot, when they attack the Enemy that are posted behind Intrenchments or Ditches, especially after they have got within them; and how is it possible to be avoided, when perhaps the Enemy may have two or three Ditches to retire to, and we pursuing after this confus'd Manner? And suppose that we drove the Enemy out of all their Cover, and are pursuing them into a Plain; the first Thing we are to do is to put ourselves in Order, left the Enemy's Horse seeing us in Confusion, come and cut us to Pieces. Wherefore when the Colonel finds the Action he's going upon, is like to occasion this Disorder, he apprizes the Battalion of it, and bids them mind their Colours, and keep as close to them as possible. The Colours

Colours ought to be carry'd by *strong Men*, and kept always well advanced, to whom the Colonel gives strict Orders to stick close by him, whatever Way he takes; he also orders two or three of the ablest Drummers, or more, to keep close by him, and at the same Time acquaints both Officers and Soldiers, that whenever they hear the Drums beat to Arms, they immediately repair to their Colours, and whatever Way they find them draw up, or front, they are to range. When the Colonel is for forming the Battalion, he orders the Colours to draw up at their proper Distance the Way he would have the Battalion front, and then ordering the Drums to beat to Arms, the Officers by whom the Battalion is to be guided, immediately range to their proper Distance on each Side the Colours. The Officers Rank being thus form'd, the Soldiers knowing on which Side the Colours they are of, and the Officers they follow, will soon fall into their Places, and the Battalion be form'd in a shorter time than can be imagin'd, that is, when they are once thoroughly acquainted with the Manner. When several Battalions happen to intermingle, as upon these Occasions often happens, the Commanding Officers inclining with their Colours, and Drums beating towards that Part where their Station is to be, will soon bring all into Order. The Major, Adjutant, and Serjeants are to bestir themselves on this Occasion; and when the Battalion is thus form'd, the Officers and Serjeants may soon fall into their Platoons, and the Lieutenant-Colonel and other Officers take their Posts in the Rear.

To DEFEND *a* BREACH *or* ENTRENCHMENT,

Which is perform'd by what we call the Parapet-firing. This, in time of Peace, is wholly laid aside,

Regiment of FOOT *upon* ACTION.

on account of its irregular Firing, and its not making a Figure on our Reviews: However, as it often falls in our Way in Time of War, I think it ought not to be neglected, but practis'd by all Battalions sometimes, tho' upon Reviews it may be omitted, unless the General require it. In this Case our Battalion will be drawn up Six deep, and the Files at such a Distance, as those that fire may have room to load before it comes to their turn to fire again. The Ranks are to keep at two good Paces distance, that the Soldiers may have room to be loading while they keep moving forward. Officers are to be posted in the front Rank, each of them to have six or eight File, at most, under their Command; and in the Interval behind each Officer, as many Officers as can be allow'd, to take Care that the Soldiers keep their Distance and Order, and hand them up from one to the other, till they come to the Officers. The remaining Part of the Officers are to be posted in the Rear, to see that the Soldiers perform their Duty, and avoid falling into Confusion. The Colonel gets the most convenient Place he can, for having a View of the Action; the Lieutenant-Colonel, Major, and Adjutant are to keep moving about all Parts, to prevent Confusion or Hurry; the Drums to keep out of the Way. When the Enemy begins the Attack, the Officers in the Front, without waiting for Orders, or staying for one another, give the Word to the Front Rank to make ready, which being done, he advances with them up to the Parapet, and then gives the Word, *Present*. In this they must be very careful, that the Soldiers point their Arms down to the Enemy, or they will be apt to fire over their Heads; he then gives the Word, *Fire*; which having done, they immediately recover their Arms, and face, upon their right Heels, to the Right about, which bring them opposite the Intervals of Fire they are to pafs through, and then they march briſkly, keeping their Arms well recover'd, until they pafs the Rear Rank two Paces; then they face again, on the right Heels, to the Right about, which brings them oppofite the Rear of their own Files; and then, and not before, they fall to loading, in which they muſt be fure to ram down their Cartridges, or they will be apt to drop out when they come to prefent briſkly down to the Enemy.

Upon the Front Rank's advancing up to the Parapet, the fecond Rank marches up to their Ground, and then makes ready, without waiting the Word of Command, where a Serjeant ſtands to fee them do it, and to hand them up to the Officer. Thus when the Front Rank has fir'd, the Second marches up to the Parapet, where the Officer ſtands to receive them, and give the Word, *Prefent*, and *Fire*; by which a conſtant Fire will be maintain'd, and the whole Battalion in conſtant Motion, and with due Care may be kept in very good Order. There are fome who, in performing this Fire, are for having the Ranks, when they have fir'd, to face all to the Right, and to march after one another to the Interval where the Officer ſtands; but this takes up too much Time, becaufe the next Rank cannot mount the Parapet till the laſt Man has got off, which makes a Stop in the Firing, and certainly is moſt ſubjeʃt to Confufion, particularly in taking up their Files, when they come to the Rear, and the Ranks clofe on each other.

I ſhall only touch on one Thing more, and conclude.

The Army now abounds moſt with young Officers, that have not feen any Thing of Aʃtion, of whom, in Courfe, the Whole muſt be compos'd; wherefore my Defign is to inform thofe Gentlemen, how they are to behave when they come to have feparate Commands,

Regiment of FOOT *upon* ACTION.

mands, and particularly in marching a Battalion or large Detachment from one Garrison to another, or on such Occasions. We have had several gallant * Officers of long Experience, yet thro' Neglect have had their Regiments or Detachments cut to pieces, and themselves kill'd, or shamefully taken, as they have been marching from one Garrison to another, and that by inconsiderable Parties of Horse, that durst not have look'd them in the Face, had they kept that due Order in their March they ought to have done. Now, to guard against the like Misfortune, and caution all young Gentlemen, who in time may have the like Command, never to think themselves over-secure upon any Duty or Command whatever, especially when there is the least Possibility of an Enemy coming to them; because the Lives of so many Men, and their own Honour, which is much more valuable than Life, as also the Service of the Country, depends wholly upon their Care and Conduct upon all those Commands: and let them not depend too much upon the Care and Judgment of others; for whatever Misfortune happens, the Blame will be laid at their Door,

I will suppose our Battalion to be in Winter-Quarters, and that the Governor has receiv'd Orders to send our Regiment, or a strong Detachment to reinforce one of our Frontier-Garrisons, or perhaps, to escort Provisions or Stores thither; this being a Thing very common in Time of War, the which ought to be managed with Caution and Prudence; for the Enemy never wants having Intelligence of those Things; and, if possible, they'll send out a Party of Horse to intercept us on our March: wherefore the Governor, if he has the least Apprehension of Danger, seldom lets his Orders be known

* Col. *Babington*, &c.

till

till the Ports are shut, and the Keys brought to him; then he gives out his Orders for the Battalion to be on the Parade by Break of Day next Morning. 'Tis probable our young Gentlemen will think these sudden Orders very hard: but whoever they are that take the Prosecution on them, must be ready to march at a Moment's Warning.

Our Battalion on the Parade at the Time appointed, the Colonel and all the Officers must not fail to be there at the same time, in order to get out of the Ports as soon as possible, as well to prevent the Men's drinking Drams, as for getting early on the March. The Battalion being ready, the Governor orders the Ports to be open'd, and the Colonel marches out, and draws up again on the Parade, where he's to make a Disposition for his March with all the Dispatch he can, by first drawing out his Advance and Rear-Guards, and then forms his Battalion or Detachment: but, as they are to fall into their March, neither Officers nor Serjeants fall into their Platoons until Occasion offers; this being done, the Colonel sends off the Advanc'd Guard, the Officer of which is to take Care that he does not keep at too great a Distance, nor yet too near the Battalion; three or four hundred Paces over a Plain will be sufficient, but less within Inclosures. He's to look often behind him to observe the March of the Battalion, and to halt when they halt; and when he has got at a little Distance, he then sends off a Serjeant and twelve Men, who are to keep about half the Distance before him as he does from the Battalion, who is also to look often behind him to see that he keeps within Sight of his Officers. They are both to be very careful in looking about them, especially when they come near any Cover, or Rising-Grounds; and if the Serjeant makes any Discovery of the Enemy,

he

he is to fire a Shot, or two, or three, and then retire to his Officer; upon which the Officer is to halt, and acquaint the Colonel; and when the Serjeant has join'd him, if he finds the Enemy advance, he is to retire to the Battalion, and observe such Orders as he shall receive from the Colonel. And as 'tis hardly possible for any but Horse to come to intercept us upon this Occasion, so the Colonel prepares to form the Square, as hereafter shewn.

So soon as the Colonel has sent off his Advance-Guard, he orders the Officer of the Rear-Guard to take Care of the Baggage, or Convoy, and see that they keep good Order in their March, and close to the Regiment. This Officer is also to detach a Serjeant and twelve Men to keep at a proper Distance in the Rear of him, and both of them to look sharp left the Enemy may lye in Ambush by the Advance-Guard, and come out, in hopes of surprizing us in the Rear, they having no Business to think of attacking us, but by surprizing us on a disorderly March. Nor is it to be conceiv'd what a Panick seizes a Body of Foot when they are surpriz'd after such a manner; nothing but Confusion attends them on such Occasions, and they are cut to Pieces before they can get into Order. Nor, on the other Hand, can it be conceiv'd with what Courage and Resolution a Body of Foot will be animated, when they find themselves in good Order, and Posture of Defence.

The Colonel having dispos'd Matters as above, and given strict Orders to both Officers and Soldiers, that they keep good Order in their March, and not stir from their Divisions, he then marches off in grand Divisions three deep, if the Ground will permit; if not, in half Ranks, which will contain two Platoons; and if the Ground will not admit of that,
he

he then subdivides into Quarter-Ranks, or single Platoons, but never into less: and if he should come to a narrow Pass, or Defile, which will not allow of our marching thus, then the half Ranks of the Platoons double to the Right behind each other; for we are by no Means to break our Platoons any otherwise; and whenever the Ground will admit, they are to march immediately out, and form their Platoons; and as the Ground enlarges, they are to double up into half Ranks, which is the easiest Way of marching: But, if there is any Apprehension of Danger, we are then to march up in grand Divisions, wherever the Ground will allow of it. Note, that the Army always marches six deep; but as we are, on this Occasion, in Danger of being attack'd by Horse, so we are to march in the readiest Posture for forming the Square, or drawing up in Battalion.

Let us suppose our Battalion on the March in grand Divisions over a Plain, with a Drum in the Front-Division, and another in the Rear, beating a March; the Divisions keeping at such Distance as they may have Room to wheel in, either for forming the Battalion, or Square. While we are thus on the March, we will suppose the Colonel has an Account ('tis no Matter whether from Front or Rear) that a Body of Horse are advancing towards us; he orders the Drums to cease beating, and the Battalion to halt; on which the Drum of the first Division comes out to him, he then gives the Word, TAKE CARE TO FORM *the* SQUARE; *and immediately after orders the* DRUM *to* BEAT *a* RUFFLE; *upon which the second Division* WHEELS *to the* RIGHT, *by the Right-Hand-Man of the first Rank, until their three Ranks on the Left* JOIN *the three Files on the* RIGHT *of the first Division; the third Division*

MARCHES *brisky, until they come to the Ground of the* SECOND, *and then they begin their Wheel to the* LEFT *by the* LEFT-HAND-MAN *of the* REAR-RANK; *and when they have made their Wheel they edge to the* RIGHT, *till their three Files on the Right take up the three Ranks on the Left of the first; and the Rear-Division all this While marches briskly, and takes the Ground from whence the second wheel'd, joining their three Ranks on the Right to the three Files on the Right of the second; and the three Files on their Left take up the three Ranks on the Left of the third, which closes the Square.* All which, with a little Practice, will be perform'd in a short Time. And in Case the Enemy should be so near as to attempt falling on us while we are forming, the Grenadiers, with the Advance and Rear Guards, are to join, and make Head against them, which will stop any Body of Horse that can possibly be sent out on such Occasions; and when our Square is form'd, the Enemy dare not venture upon us, since they could not surprize us on a disorderly March, which is all the Sign we are to apprehend. Nor has it been known that any on the like Occasion did ever miscarry, but by the Carelessness and Neglect of the Commanding Officers, who have had Tails on their March some Miles long.

THE BAGGAGE must by no Means come into the Square, nor will there be any Danger of it. If they do but keep close to the Square, the Grenadiers, with the Advance and Rear-Guards, will be sufficient to take Care of them. THE ENEMY, when they find us in this Posture of Defence, will soon make off, lest our Frontiers hearing of their being abroad, might send out a superior Force to intercept them. However, we are to continue our March in the Square,

DISCIPLINE *for a*

till we get over the Plain, and come up with inclosed Grounds, where the Horse have no Business to come near us; and being come up to those Grounds, we must reduce the Square before they enter them; whereupon the Colonel halts the Battalion, and then gives the Word, TAKE CARE to *reduce the Square.*

NOTE, *That upon Halting we are not to Face Square, but continue as we were on the March, till the Drum beats a* RUFFLE; *on which the Rear-Division face to the* RIGHT-ABOUT; *the third face to the* RIGHT, *and edge away, to get clear to the Right of the Front Division, and the second face to the* LEFT; *and upon beating the Flam, the Rear-Division marches forward, the third wheels to the* RIGHT *by the same Man they wheel'd on before; and when they have made half their Wheel, the second begins their Wheel to the* LEFT *by the same Man they wheel'd on before. When the third Division has made theirs, they march forward after the fourth, to give Room to the second; and when the Major and Adjutant find, that the third and fourth Divisions have got to their proper Distance, and the second made their Wheel, they acquaint the Colonel of it, who then orders his Drum to beat a* RUFFLE; *upon which the three Divisions in the Rear* FACE *all to the* LEFT-ABOUT; *and upon the Drum's beating a* MARCH, *the whole Battalion marches off at once*; and on our entring the enclosed Grounds, we are then to march as the Roads will admit: And tho' we have got clear of the Horse, yet we must still be on our Guard against an Ambuscade. Wherefore we should be much more careful in marching thro' these Grounds, than over the Plain. And tho' it may seem impossible that a sufficient Body of Foot could be sent from the Enemy's Frontiers to way-lay us, yet as they always have a Number of Partizan Parties abroad, who may hear of our March, and so draw together,

gether, and lie hid in some close Cover; and though they durst not openly attempt us, yet if they find us on a careless March, may throw in among us, which would certainly put us under great Confusion; and 'tis hard to say what may be the Consequence; for I have known some of these impudent Fellows, that have lain hid in a Wood, fire upon the Skirt of our Grand Army, as we have been on the March: Wherefore, I say, great Care must be taken in marching thro' inclosed Grounds, where both the Advance and Rear-Guards ought to be more circumspect in looking about them, and send Men off on every Side, to inspect into all suspected Covers. AND THEREFORE I cannot help recommending that most commendable Part of an Officer, of being diligent on all Duties and Commands, and not to trust to others, as I have too often seen among our *English* Gentlemen; and am sorry to say, that I have not known, among all the Nations I have served with, any Officers so remiss on Duty, as the Generality of our Countrymen; who, in other Respects, not only equal, but in a great measure excell. And why should this supine Negligence blast those other heroick Qualifications? And certainly, whenever a Gentleman takes the Profession of Arms upon him, he ought to study all Parts of it, from the Centinel to the General: For there is nothing will recommend him more to his Prince, or General, than that of being known to be an expert and diligent Officer, the which has raised Numbers of Men from private Centinels, to be General Officers; when those who have commanded them, have been at a Stand, and obliged to make their Court to them.

Thus have I gone through these Rules of Discipline, where I hope Hints will be found, that have not yet been touch'd on by any of our modern *Martinets*.

It

It may be expected that I should say something of the Behaviour of an Army in general; but that being an Affair that I can't pretend to, nor is it possible for the greatest General to prescribe certain Rules for fighting an Army; the Situation of Ground, the various Turns and unforeseen Accidents, which frequently and unavoidably attend all Battles, especially when an Enemy do obstinately dispute every Inch of Ground, are Things greatly depending on the ready Genius and Conduct of the General, and the Goodness of the Troops he commands. Besides, in that of one Army attacking another, there is something unaccountable in it; for though the Army attack'd has the Advantage of Ground which they have made Choice of, and very often more numerous in Troops, yet it is rarely known, but the Army which attacks does assuredly get the Victory.

F I N I S.

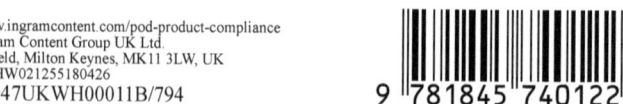